BookMarks

Volume 3

BookMarks

Volume 3

Bible Explorations for Older Youth

Edited by
Grace Burton-Edwards

Judson Press ■ Valley Forge

Library of Congress Cataloging-in-Publication Data

Bible explorations for older youth / edited by Grace Burton-Edwards.

   p.   cm.

Volume 3: ISBN 0-8170-1333-4 (pbk. : alk. paper)

Volume 2: ISBN 0-8170-1332-6 (pbk. : alk. paper)

Volume 1: ISBN 0-8170-1331-8 (pbk. : alk. paper)

1. Bible—Study and teaching.   2. Christian education of young people.   I. Burton-Edwards, Grace.   II. Series: Bookmarks (Judson Press) ; v. 3.

BS600.2.B443 1999

220′.071′2—dc21   99-36852

Printed in the U.S.A.

06 05 04 03 02 01 00

10 9 8 7 6 5 4 3 2 1

Contents

~~~~~~~~

Welcome to *BookMarks,* a fresh idea in Bible study curriculum for older youth. *BookMarks* combines a high regard for the biblical story with respect for the honesty and thoughtfulness of older youth. The sixteen sessions in this volume are specifically designed to give youth access to the Bible in a way that challenges youth to discover meaning in the Bible for their own lives. You'll notice the difference right away!

BookMarks is designed as an elective series for older youth, and may be used independently of other curricula or as a part of the larger curriculum series, *Bible Quest: A Bible Story Curriculum for All Ages,* with which it is affiliated. As part of the *Bible Quest* series, each volume of *BookMarks* will consider four broad themes that emerge from the biblical story. These are: Covenant, Salvation, Liberation and Justice, and Incarnation. In addition, each *BookMarks* volume will contain one unit suitable for either Advent/Christmas or Lent/Easter. As an elective series, *BookMarks* sessions can easily be used in a number of Bible study settings, including Sunday school, youth group sessions, and retreats.

The Story Is the Point

One of the greatest challenges for the church today is how to address the biblical illiteracy of young people who have grown up in the church. Many youth who have spent years in Sunday school and youth programs remember little about what is in the Bible. Although the Bible has been used to teach many lessons, youth seem to have missed the story behind the message—end of lesson, end of story! For *BookMarks,* the biblical story *is* the point! The objective of each session is to create an opportunity for youth to engage the story directly, so that the biblical story itself is what is remembered. Through this direct encounter with the Bible, the Bible story is joined to the story of our own lives, challenging our behavior, informing our decisions, and nurturing relationship with God.

The Learner Is an Interpreter

BookMarks values the perspectives youth bring to their study of the Bible. Each session encourages youth to see the biblical story in the light of their own lives. In addition, each session provides an opportunity for youth to practice using tools and approaches that contribute to responsible interpretation. As youth become familiar with the process of biblical interpretation, they are encouraged to consider the Bible an accessible resource for faith and life. As youth are able to see the connections between their own story and the biblical story, they discover meaning in that story and learn to look to Scripture as a resource for living now and in the future.

A Six-Step Process

The sessions in *BookMarks* use a six-step process to help youth engage the Bible story and find meaning in that story for their lives. Each step includes two options, so the leader can design the session especially for the needs of the youth. In "Setting the Stage," youth are welcomed into the interpretive process through activities and discussions that foreshadow key features of the story to be considered. In "Telling the Story," the story itself is presented in ways that will help youth to pay close attention to its plot, characters, and content. In "Reacting to the Story," youth are invited and helped to share their initial responses to the story, including their questions and their first impressions of its meaning. In "Connecting to the Story," youth are challenged to discover the intersection of the biblical story with their own lives, seeing themselves through the characters and situations of the Bible story and beginning to identify the personal relevance of the story. In "Exploring the Story," youth are introduced to various tools and approaches for responsible biblical interpretation, encouraging them to place their own understanding of the story in the context of the wider faith community. In "Living the Story," youth express their emerging sense of the meaning of the story for their lives in a closing context of affirmation and worship. In addition, each *BookMarks* session includes two reproducible handouts designed to contribute to the learning process.

Additional Features

In addition to the six-step process with two options in each step, *Book-Marks* sessions include a number of other features to support the leader in the process of helping youth discover the relevance of Scripture for their lives. "A Story behind the Story" provides the leader with contextual information about the biblical story, describing important historical, cultural, and theological backgrounds to the story. "Possible Youth Contact Points" suggests some of the issues and questions important to youth that may become avenues of connection to the biblical story. "You May Need" provides an up-front look at the materials you may need to gather depending on the session options you choose. "Enter the Story" suggests a process for the leader's intentional engagement with the Bible story prior to leading the session, encouraging reflection that may contribute to the interpretive process. "Things to Ponder" helps the leader to be aware of possible issues for youth that may emerge or need further attention as a result of studying a particular Bible story. "Looking Ahead" helps the leader to anticipate those options in the next session that may need some extra preparation time.

The Editor of This Volume

Grace Burton-Edwards has been a youth minister, confirmation teacher, curriculum writer, and workshop leader for many years. She is currently part of the ministry staff of First United Methodist Church in Anderson, Indiana, where she leads seeker worship and community ministries at the congregation's second campus site. In addition to serving as editor of this volume, Grace has written for Volumes 1 and 4 of *BookMarks*.

The Writers of This Volume

Dotty Abney is the minister of Christian education and youth programs at First Christian Church in Richardson, Texas. As an experienced minister with youth, she has developed and written curriculum for her local church for many years.

David Adams is an American Baptist minister who has worked for many years in youth and young adult ministry. An experienced curriculum writer and editor, he previously contributed to *BookMarks, Volume 1*. David currently serves as associate pastor of Central Baptist Church in Lexington, Kentucky.

Kissa Hamilton is an ordained elder in the United Methodist Church with extensive experience as a curriculum writer for youth. Kissa is currently serving as the minister with youth and their families at First United Methodist Church in Grapevine, Texas.

Steven B. Lawrence currently serves as administrative assistant to the pastor at the White Rock Baptist Church in Philadelphia, Pennsylvania, and is an adjunct professor at Eastern Baptist Theological Seminary in Wynnewood, Pennsylvania. An American Baptist minister, he has participated in the development and leadership of national youth conferences for many years. Steven also contributed to Volume 1 of the *BookMarks* series.

It is my sincere hope that you and your youth will enjoy these sixteen sessions as a fresh opportunity to consider the biblical story as full of meaning for our lives.

Grace and peace to you in Christ,

Thom

J. Thomas Son, Managing Editor
Board of Educational Ministries
American Baptist Churches, USA

1. In the Beginning

Bible Story: Genesis 1:1–2:4

A Story behind the Story

"Genesis" means beginning, and the Book of Genesis contains not one but two stories of beginning. Sacred to at least three of the world's great religions, these accounts of the beginnings of time reflect the finest traditions of storytelling. The text for this session, Genesis 1:1–2:4, is one of these accounts. The other is found in Genesis 2:4 and following.

The differences between the two stories are interesting. In Genesis 1, creation takes place in six distinct days. God speaks creation into being, beginning with the creation of light in the midst of the formless void. Living creatures are made on the fifth day. Human beings (male and female) are made at the same time on the sixth day. God rests on the seventh day. In Genesis 2:4 and following, God hand-forms creation in an unspecified amount of time. Adam is made first. After creating Adam, God plants a garden and fills it with living creatures, including Eve, who is like Adam. God's words seem more like conversation than creative pronouncement. The two stories are very different, yet both testify that the universe had a definite starting point and that God was and is the power behind creation.

Biblical scholars believe that the passage used in this session is from a later time than the version found in Genesis 2:4 and following. It may have been recorded by members of the "priestly" tradition in ancient Israel, meaning that it likely comes from a time when religious practice was well organized and ritualized. The Genesis 2 passage reflects an earlier time, when stories of God would have been repeated around a campfire rather than in a formal worship setting. This distinction could explain why this version of the story is more thorough and dramatic than the Genesis 2 story. This is a passage of Scripture that was meant to be read aloud to an audience, perhaps an audience at worship. The words found here, especially in the original Hebrew, have a rhythm and majesty that draw listeners into the drama of creation. But it is the wonder of the story itself that empowers this saga—God speaking all things into being and making human beings in God's own image.

Enter the Story

Find a time and place where you can read the story and consider it. Bring paper and pencil with you to note any questions or observations you might have. Read the story, making notes as you proceed. Read the story again and consider how your own story is related to this ancient one. Make notes about these thoughts too.

Take a moment to remember what it was like to have a story read to you. What were the things that made the experience come alive for you? How can you help draw the youth into this experience in ways that will move them as well? In your own mind, you will need to deal with some of the serious questions surrounding this passage of Scripture. How do you feel about

Section One

Incarnation
by David Adams

POSSIBLE YOUTH CONTACT POINTS

- Where did all this come from?
- How did early believers understand the story of creation?
- What is the "creationism versus evolution" debate about?
- What is my place in the overall scheme of God's creation?
- What does God's creating nature tell me about God?
- Why are people here?

YOU MAY NEED

- examples of creative process (see "Setting the Stage")
- paper and pencils
- newsprint and markers
- Bibles
- objects corresponding to days of creation (see "Telling the Story," Option B)
- paper, pipe cleaners, or modeling clay
- "Make a World!" handouts
- several different translations of the Bible
- Bible study tools like commentaries or study Bibles
- "I Have a Dream" handouts or audio recording of Dr. King's speech and a way to play it

the idea of taking this account of creation literally? How does your opinion of God's creative process affect the way you come to this story? If you have the time, listen to pieces of music about God's creation and consider incorporating them into this session.

Pray and think deeply on this story before you go to help others experience it.

Setting the Stage (10 minutes)

Needed: tools or examples of any kind of creative process—hammer and nails, pen and paper, art supplies, building plans, and so on

Before the session starts, prepare the meeting space by placing various tools of exploration and creation in strategic spots. As participants arrive, encourage them to look at the supplies you've brought. As they gravitate toward things that they find most familiar or interesting, ask them about their choices and about what is going on in their lives. How was the week? Are there any concerns they would like to share?

OPTION A

As you get ready to consider today's story from the Bible, ask for volunteers to share a story about a time when they felt proud of something they made—objects they constructed with their hands, stories they wrote, music they performed, and the like. Encourage them to talk about what they made and why; how their creation was planned; where, when, and with whom they created it; and what was done with their creation afterwards. Invite the other youth to talk

with them if they have made similar things. After everyone who wishes to share a story has spoken, discuss as a group the reasons that some creations bring their creators a great deal of pride, while others are taken for granted.

OPTION B

Needed: paper, pencils, newsprint, markers

Form pairs or triads. Distribute paper and pencils to each team and invite them to make a list of what they believe are the five most important creations of the past fifty years. Let the teams know that they are free to choose any creations or inventions they wish, tangible (objects) or intangible (ideas), as long as the team is unanimous in its choices and can provide a rationale for each one.

Give the teams about five minutes to discuss their choices. Then call time and invite the teams to share their top-five lists with the rest of the group. Select a volunteer to make a master list of inventions as they are read, placing check marks next to those that are chosen multiple times. After all the choices are shared, discuss the master list. What items on the list are the most debatable? least debatable? What other items should be on the list? What, if anything, do the youth know of the stories behind the creation of the items of the list?

Telling the Story (10–15 minutes)

OPTION A
Needed: Bibles

Arrange chairs in a circle, facing outward, and invite participants to sit. Tell them that you are about to read a story and that you will need help providing dramatic effects. To select helpers, ask the group to walk silently around the outside of the circle while you read the passages aloud. When you stop reading, everyone must find a seat immediately. Whoever cannot find a seat will make a noise or dramatic gesture that best summarizes what occurred in the Scripture that was read.

After making sure that everyone understands the procedure (musical chairs without the music), remove one chair from the circle and begin. Read Genesis 1:1–5 as the youth walk around. At the conclusion of the reading, have the person who is standing create a dramatic effect for that day. Repeat the process for each day, removing a chair each time. After the sixth day (1:31), return all chairs to a circle facing in and read the passage for the final day (2:1–4a). Invite everyone to dramatize that passage by sitting down. (If you have a small group, use the same process, but do not remove an additional chair for each day. Play all the rounds with one less chair than you have people.)

OPTION B
Needed: objects that correspond to each day of creation: for example, a bright flashlight, a container of water, a leafy plant, moon and stars, a small live or toy animal, and so on
Invite the group to sit in a circle. Make the room as dark as possible and tell the group that the story you are about to relate has been told for thousands of years. Encourage them to tune out any outside interference as they listen to the story.

When everyone is settled in, read or invite a volunteer to read Genesis 1:1–2:4a. As you read, pass the objects that correspond to each day around the circle. (For instance, when you read, "Let there be light," turn on the bright flashlight and pass it around. When you read about the waters, pass a container of water around the circle, and so on.) Read the passages slowly and clearly, allowing time for everyone to touch each object before hearing about the next day. At the conclusion of the reading, invite the group to rest and consider the story. Remain silent for about thirty seconds. Then turn on the lights.

Reacting to the Story (10 minutes)
OPTION A
Needed: scrap paper and pencils
Ask the group to imagine that they have been given the opportunity to travel back in time to the very beginning of creation for five minutes. They may choose any point in the process of creation described in the passage they just read, but they may make only one trip, and they may stay there only five minutes. Allow a few moments for the participants to decide how they would respond to that opportunity. Then invite them to talk about which moment they would choose and why.

Note: Some youth may say that they cannot imagine going back to a point in time described in this passage. Some may not believe that creation happened this way and may prefer to go back to a "big bang" or some other theorized beginning point. Others may say that they believe that this account of creation should not be taken literally but understood as a description of how things might have happened. If the participants seem uncomfortable with the activity, use their discomfort as an opportunity to talk about the tension that exists between scientific accounts of creation and biblical accounts of creation. These feelings are appropriate reactions to this story.

When everyone who wants to share has had a chance to do so, distribute paper and pencils and invite the participants to write one question they would like to ask God about creation. After they have written their questions, have them fold up their papers and place them in a pile.

OPTION B
Needed: modeling clay, or paper, or pipe cleaners
Ask the youth to think about the object or image from this story that most stands out in their minds. Then give them each some Play-Doh™ or modeling clay and invite them to make the object or a representation of the image that they have in mind. If these are not easily accessible, invite youth to make a sculpture out of pipe cleaners or tear paper into a shape that represents a significant image for them. After a few minutes, or when everyone appears to have finished, encourage a few volunteers to share what they made and why they made it.

Connecting to the Story (10–15 minutes)
OPTION A
Needed: questions from "Reacting to the Story," Option A
This exercise follows Option A under "Reacting to the Story."

Place one chair in front of the rest of the group and announce that this is "God's seat." Invite one of the youth to play the part of God for a few moments. If no one is willing to sit in God's seat, begin the process by playing the part of God yourself. Distribute the questions from the pile, being careful that the participants receive a question other than their own. Ask for a volunteer to read a question to the person sitting in "God's seat." Whoever is playing the part of God should try to answer the question as she or he believes God would answer it. Encourage the participants to ask questions about this response. Does everyone believe that God would answer the question this way? What are other possible responses? Continue playing, allowing others who wish to do so to play the part of God. If time permits, try to deal with all of the questions.

OPTION B
Needed: pencils, "Make a World!" handouts
Give each person a pencil and a copy of the "Make a World!" handout. Allow about five minutes for the participants to read and complete it. Then form teams of no more than three people and ask them to compare and discuss their handouts. After about five minutes, or when the conversation appears to be dying down, call time and ask for volunteers from the entire group to talk about what they found they had in common with the other members of their team. Ask the participants what they learned about their world from doing this. What are the most significant ways in which the worlds they would like

to create would differ from the one that God created, and why do they differ?

If you are choosing Option B in "Living the Story," keep these sheets for future reference.

Exploring the Story (10–15 minutes)

OPTION A

Needed: paper, Bibles, pencils

Ask the participants to form groups of two or three. Distribute paper and pencils and ask the youth to create a checklist for God for each day of creation. What did God do or say on Day 1, Day 2, and so on? Encourage them to be as specific as possible. When they complete their lists, ask the participants if they see any patterns to what God was doing. Use these lists as a basis for talking about what God did in creation. Then ask how God's work at the time of creation is similar to God's work today:

■ Is God still creating things?
■ What does God say and do today?
■ What sort of world does God want to see?
■ What is God creating in our lives?

OPTION B

Needed: several different translations of the Bible, Bible study tools such as commentaries or study Bibles

Provide several different translations of the Bible, including traditional versions such as the King James Version and contemporary translations such as the Contemporary English Version or *The Message*. Distribute these Bibles and ask volunteers to read portions of

Genesis 1:1–2:4 aloud. Ask the participants to pay attention to words and phrases that are translated differently and to pay special attention to the sixth day of creation. When most of the story has been read, have the participants divide into groups of three or four. Ask the groups to rewrite Genesis 1:26–31 in contemporary language. Suggest that they read commentaries or use other Bible study tools to help them discover the meaning of these verses. When the groups have completed their paraphrases, invite them to read them aloud. Then talk about what these verses mean, using questions like these:

■ In what ways are we like God?
■ What sort of relationship does God want humans to have with the rest of creation?
■ How does God feel about us?
■ How does God feel about creation in general?

Living the Story (5 minutes)

OPTION A

Needed: "I Have a Dream" handouts or an audio recording of the speech

Have the participants form a circle and tell them that many people of faith believe that they have a responsibility to help create a world that is more faithful to their creator's vision than the one in which we currently reside. It is this impulse that drives people to dream great dreams and strive to rise above the forces of destruction around us.

Invite members of the group to consider and then discuss the one thing that they would most like to see happen in order to make the world a better place. After the participants have had some time to talk it over, lead them, in turn, to complete this sentence: "My dream is to help create a world where—"

At the conclusion of the sharing, tell the group that one of the most famous speeches of this century is Martin Luther King Jr.'s "I Have a Dream" speech, in which he shared a vision for the world he wanted to help God create. The copy included on the handout includes the responses given by the audience when the speech was first presented. Invite the participants to read these responses during the reading of the speech to create the feeling of what it must have been like to hear Dr. King deliver it. Close with a prayer that we may all work to realize God's dreams for creation.

OPTION B
Needed: newsprint, markers, used "Make a World!" handouts
Give two volunteers markers and ask them to stand at a large sheet of newsprint. Tell the rest of the group that you wish to end the session by creating, as a group, a vision of the "ideal" word. As the group shares its vision of the ideal world, the volunteers should draw or list each item introduced. Start by referring to the "Make a World!" handouts and listing or drawing those items that are common to more than one sheet. Then move to other ideas that individuals think are important. As each individual item is introduced, have the participant sharing it explain his or her reasoning.

When the group runs out of suggestions, ask "What do you think you can or should do to make this kind of world a reality?" After a few volunteers have shared, close with a prayer that all will find the strength and opportunity to help bring about the world that they envision.

Things to Ponder
This passage is sometimes a source of controversy in the church. It would be very easy to get caught up in a creationism-versus-evolution debate as one reads it. Some Christians view this passage as a story about God's act in creation, not as a description of precisely how God created. For others, however, this passage brings up confusing and conflicting claims of modern science versus ancient understandings. It is important, therefore, to avoid pushing people into corners as they relate to this passage of Scripture. Give God room to work.

Looking Ahead
The next session focuses on the story of Elijah on Mount Horeb, as found in 1 Kings 19:1–18. Since it concerns itself in part with the distance between God and us, you might wish to prepare in advance by finding music that addresses that subject. You might also wish to gather some noise-making equipment for use in Option A of "Telling the Story," which is meant to be staged like an old-time radio broadcast.

Make a World!

This is your big chance to play God for a day (you know you want to). In the space below, make a list or sketches of the changes that you'd make if you had the power to create the world of your choice. Just remember to rest when you're done!

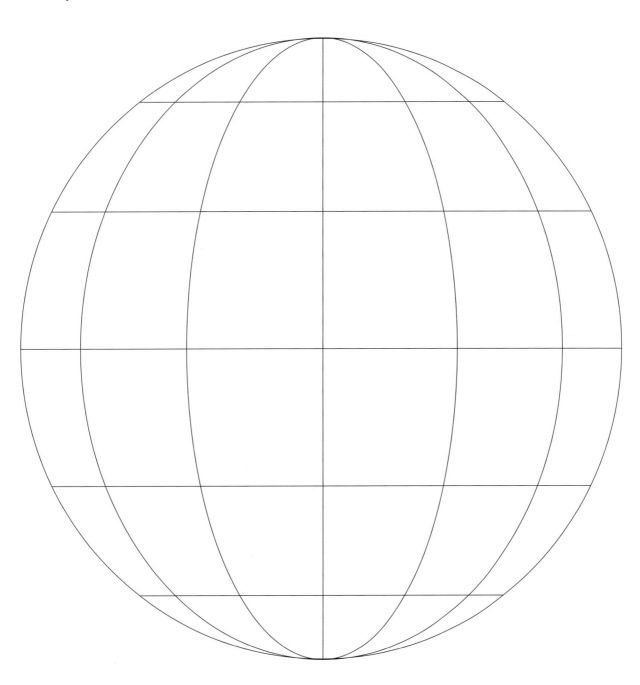

I Have a Dream

Martin Luther King Jr.

I say to you today, my friends, [*Applause*] so even though we face the difficulties of today and tomorrow, I still have a dream. (*Yes*) It is a dream deeply rooted in the American dream.

I have a dream that one day (*Yes*) this nation will rise up and live out the true meaning of its creed: "We hold these truths to be self-evident, that all men are created equal." (*Yes*) [*Applause*]

I have a dream that one day on the red hills of Georgia, the sons of former slaves and the sons of former slave owners will be able to sit down together at the table of brotherhood.

I have a dream that one day even the state of Mississippi, a state sweltering with the heat of injustice, (*Well*) sweltering with the heat of oppression, will be transformed into an oasis of freedom and justice.

I have a dream (*Well*) [*Applause*] that my four little children will one day live in a nation where they will not be judged by the color of their skin but by the content of their character. (*My Lord*)

I have a dream today! [*Applause*]

I have a dream that one day down in Alabama, with its vicious racists (*Yes*)—with its governor having his lips dripping with the words of interposition and nullification—(*Yes*) one day right there in Alabama little black boys and black girls will be able to join hands with little white boys and white girls as sisters and brothers.

I have a dream today! [*Applause*]

I have a dream that one day "every valley shall be exalted (*Yes*) and every hill and mountain shall be made low. The rough places will be made plain and the crooked places will be made straight, (*Yes*) and the glory of the Lord shall be revealed, and all flesh shall see it together." (*Yes*)

This is our hope. This is the faith that I go back to the South with. (*Yes*) With this faith we will be able to hew out of the mountain of despair a stone of hope. With this faith (*Yes*) we will be able to transform the jangling discords of our nation into a beautiful symphony of brotherhood. (*Talk about it*) With this faith (*My Lord*) we will be able to work together, to pray together, to struggle together, to go to jail together, to stand up for freedom together, knowing that we will be free one day. [*Applause*] This will be the day, [*Applause continues*] this will be the day when all of God's children (*Yes*) will be able to sing with new meaning:

> My country, 'tis of thee, (*Yes*) sweet land of liberty, of thee I sing.
> Land where my fathers died, land of the pilgrim's pride, (*Yes*)
> From every mountainside, let freedom ring!

> And if America is to be a great nation, this must become true.
> So let freedom ring (*Yes*) from the prodigious hilltops of New Hampshire.
> Let freedom ring from the mighty mountains of New York.
> Let freedom ring from the heightening Alleghenies of Pennsylvania. (*Yes. All right*)
> Let freedom ring from the snow-capped Rockies of Colorado. (*Well*)
> Let freedom ring from the curvaceous slopes of California. (*Yes*)
> But not only that.
> Let freedom ring from Stone Mountain of Georgia. (*Yes*)
> Let freedom ring from Lookout Mountain of Tennessee. (*Yes*)
> Let freedom ring from every hill and molehill of Mississippi. [*Applause*]
> From every mountainside, [*Applause*] let freedom ring.

And when this happens, [*Applause continues*] when we allow freedom to ring, when we let it ring from every village and every hamlet, from every state and every city, (*Yes*) we will be able to speed up that day when all God's children, black men and white men, Jews and Gentiles, Protestants and Catholics, will be able to join hands and sing in the words of the old Negro spiritual:

Free at last! (*Yes*) Free at last!

Thank God Almighty, we are free at last! [*Applause*]

Source: The Martin Luther King, Jr. Papers Project at Stanford University (www.stanford.edu/group/King).

2. What Are You Doing Here?

Bible Story: 1 Kings 19:1–18

A Story behind the Story

Elijah is widely viewed as the greatest of the prophets whose deeds are related in the Hebrew Scriptures. While other biblical prophets (like Isaiah and Jeremiah) are known largely for the way they addressed issues in the lives of their people, Elijah is known largely for the miracles he performed and for his boldness in confronting political authorities. His influence was so great in that regard that many of the earliest Christian believers wondered if Jesus was Elijah reincarnated. (See Mark 8:27–30 for an example.) Jesus' advanced way of teaching, the miracles he performed, and the reaction he got from the authorities of his day have much in common with the experiences of Elijah.

This session explores an encounter Elijah had with God. Prior to this encounter, Elijah had performed a few of his more "earthshaking" miracles. First, as recorded in 1 Kings 17, Elijah confronted King Ahab and told him that God was sending a drought to punish Ahab and his wicked Queen Jezebel for turning away from the worship of God. So that Elijah could escape the drought and the wrath of the king and queen, God led him to a wilderness where ravens brought food to him. He then went to the home of a poor widow. While he lived there, her jar of grain and her vessel of oil never ran out. When her son became ill, Elijah raised him from the point of death. First Kings 18 tells us that Elijah presided over a contest on Mount Carmel between the Canaanite god Baal and Elijah's Lord Yahweh. The priests of Baal begged their god to send fire from heaven, but nothing happened. Elijah poured water on his altar, and Yahweh sent enough fire to burn even the drenched altar. Yahweh was victorious.

Elijah's actions turned King Ahab and the people back to the worship of God. The resulting loss of face led Queen Jezebel to seek to have Elijah killed. Just at the height of his success, Elijah was forced to be on the run once again. Burdened with fears and doubts, Elijah escaped into the wilderness. There, he waited for the Lord to pass by. But the Lord was not found in the form that Elijah expected.

Enter the Story

Before reading this story, try to remember a time when life's difficulties placed a strain on your relationship with God. How did you get into and out of the situation? How did you feel about God during this time? What did you want God to do? Was God near to you during this time, or did God seem far away? What did you learn from this experience that affected your relationship with God?

After considering these questions, read the information found in "A Story behind the Story." Then read 1 Kings 19:1–18. Make notes of your questions and observations as you read. What does Elijah's faith struggle have in common with

- Where can I find God?
- Where is God when things are going badly for me?
- To what levels of commitment does God call me?
- For what future is God preparing me?
- How do I know when God wants me to do something?
- Does Elijah's life struggle mean anything for me?
- What am I getting into when I decide to set myself apart to serve God?
- What am I doing here?

YOU MAY NEED

- cake
- a pitcher of water and cups
- brooms in an umbrella holder or small kitchen trash can, or a large leafy plant
- copies of the text from 1 Kings 19:1–18
- a microphone on a stand
- several noise-making devices
- markers or pens
- penlight or flashlight
- paper and pencils
- newsprint and markers
- "Elijah and Me" handouts
- commentaries and other Bible study materials
- Bibles (preferably several versions)
- "Where Is God?" handouts

yours? Have you had a similar experience with God? What experiences in the lives of the youth in your group might be similar to the difficulties Elijah faced? How might God speak to them in the midst of these difficulties?

Pray and think deeply about this story before you go to help others experience it.

Setting the Stage (10 minutes)

Needed: cake, a pitcher of water, cups, brooms in an umbrella holder or small kitchen trash can, or a large leafy plant

Before the session begins, set up a "broom tree" or a large indoor plant on a table. To make a broom tree, place several brooms upside down in an umbrella holder, small kitchen trash can, or other container. (Note: If you choose to make a broom tree, be sure to use a translation of Scripture in "Telling the Story" that uses the phrase "broom tree" in 1 Kings 19:4, such as the Revised Standard Version or the New Revised Standard Version. Some contemporary translations translate the phrase "large bush.") If you cannot make a broom tree and do not have access to a large plant, make a bush out of paper.

Set out the cake and water under the broom tree or plant. As the group gathers, talk around the table about what's happening in the lives of the youth. How was the week? What is everyone talking about? Are there any concerns anyone would like to share? Give everyone some cake and water to eat and drink as you are talking. Move on to one of the following questions.

OPTION A

If you built a broom tree, ask volunteers to hazard guesses about its significance. Ask:

- What is it?
- What do you think it represents?
- What might be its significance as a symbol of something in religion or life in general?

Do not reveal its significance in the Scripture story until you begin "Telling the Story."

OPTION B

Before beginning to tell the story for this session, encourage participants to answer the question "What are you doing here?" (Note: This phrase is found in 1 Kings 19:13 in the New Revised Standard Version. Check the translation of Scripture that you will be using in "Telling the Story," and ask the question as it appears there.) Do not provide any clarifying statements for the question as you ask it, no matter how hard-pressed you may be. Simply ask the question over and over again and encourage participants to answer as they see fit. Then ask for volunteers to explain why and in what ways that question may be an important one.

Telling the Story (10–15 minutes)

OPTION A

Needed: photocopies of the text from 1 Kings 19:1–18, a microphone on a stand, several noise-making devices, markers or pens for note taking

Place the microphone in the middle of the room and tell the group that, in the days before television, radio was the means by which people conveyed stories to a mass audience. Invite the participants to create a radio play that conveys the exciting story found in 1 Kings 19:1–18. Remind them that since no one could see what was happening on the radio, a narrator was essential. The narrator's job was to tell the audience what was happening. Radio dramas also included actors who played the various roles and sound-effects engineers who made the noises needed to bring the story to life. Remind the group that radio actors had to speak with great drama and emotion because the audience could not see their faces.

Choose volunteers to play the roles in the Scripture passage. Then encourage them to spend a few minutes preparing to present the story as a radio drama. When everyone appears to be ready, have the group act out the drama.

OPTION B
Needed: a Bible and a penlight or flashlight
Prepare in advance by setting up a very dark room or cave-like area in your meeting place. This could be a closet, a table with a blanket draped over the sides, or another dark and enclosed space. Gather the group into the "cave," and prepare them to hear the story of Elijah by asking them to imagine that they are hiding in a place like this from someone who wants to do them harm.

When everyone is in a "running and hiding" frame of mind, use a penlight or flashlight to read 1 Kings 19:1–18 to the group as slowly and dramatically as possible. If possible, use noises or vocal tones that emphasize the various elements

of the story (the wind, and so on) as you read it. Stop frequently to be sure that everyone understands what is happening in the story. Clarify as needed. When you finish reading the story, have the group remain silent for a few seconds after the reading. Then come out of the "cave."

Reacting to the Story (10 minutes)
OPTION A
Needed: markers in a variety of colors, newsprint or banner paper
Divide participants into groups of four to six. Give each group a selection of markers in a variety of colors and a large piece of newsprint or banner paper. Remind the groups that this story represents a difficult time in Elijah's life. Help the youth recall what happened to Elijah in this story. As you recall each event, talk together about how Elijah may have felt at that particular point.

When you have finished recalling the story, invite the participants to think about these experiences as if they were a roller coaster or some other amusement park ride. Ask them to work together to create a ride that helps the riders know what happened to Elijah and helps them feel what Elijah may have felt. Have them design and draw the ride on the paper that is provided. Allow about five minutes. Share designs for rides when all of the groups are ready.

OPTION B
Needed: paper and pencils
Distribute paper and pencils to the youth and ask them to think about Elijah's situation before he meets

God at Mount Horeb. Ask questions such as:
- Where is he?
- What has happened to him?
- Why is he where he is?
- How would it feel to be in that position?
- What would your fears or concerns be?

Next ask the youth to imagine that a friend has come to see Elijah while he is hiding. The friend does not want to be caught there but is willing to take a very brief note to Elijah's mother. Encourage the group to write the note as if they were Elijah, bearing in mind that it has to be brief, since their friend, who is also on the run, cannot wait for long.

After a couple of minutes, or when everyone has finished writing, invite a few volunteers to read their letters. Ask the group to identify some of the common reactions to Elijah's predicament that appear in the letters.

Connecting to the Story (10–15 minutes)

OPTION A

Needed: pencils, "Elijah and Me" handouts

Begin this activity by reminding the youth that Elijah was one of the great heroes of the Old Testament. He was so great that many people compared Jesus to Elijah. In spite of his greatness, Elijah had to deal with some of his own problems. Distribute pencils and copies of the "Elijah and Me" handout. Ask the participants to read carefully through the handout and complete it as thoroughly as possible. After

making sure that everyone in the group understands how to complete the handout, give them about five minutes to do so.

When enough time has passed, or when most of the youth appear to have finished their work, call time and form pairs. Invite the participants to share their work with their partners, explaining everything as clearly as possible. After everyone has shared, call time and invite volunteers to share their work with the large group. Talk together about this activity. Ask questions such as:
- What were some common findings from this work?
- What did you learn about yourself or others from doing this work?
- What does the story of Elijah mean to you?

OPTION B

Needed: pencils, paper

Make sure that the participants all have paper and something to write with and ask them to imagine that they are one of Elijah's parents. They have just received a brief letter from him concerning his present situation, and they are a bit concerned about him. With that in mind, have each youth write a letter to Elijah, asking any pertinent questions and offering any advice that might be useful.

After five or ten minutes, or when everyone appears to have finished, call time and invite volunteers to share their letters with the rest of the group. Ask the group to identify those questions and concerns expressed in the letters that reveal common ground between them and Elijah. What do they have in common with him? How is Elijah like some of their friends? What experiences have they had that are similar to experiences Elijah had?

Exploring the Story (10–15 minutes)

OPTION A

Needed: Bibles, commentaries and other study materials, pencils and paper

Form two or three teams and give each some paper, pencils, and a Bible. Invite the teams to imagine that they have been hired to produce documentaries about the life of Elijah. Their job is to take stories about Elijah from Scriptures and put them together in an interesting fashion that can be shown in a one-hour format. Stories about Elijah are found in 1 Kings 17–22 and 2 Kings 1–2. The teams must select what events they will include in their documentaries, keeping in mind that the show's length can be no more than an hour. The main goal is for them to do good research and to outline their findings in a way that allows them to prepare an interesting presentation. Encourage the teams to use their Bibles as well as biblical research materials for preparing their documentaries.

After about ten minutes, or when the teams have finished, call time and have teams share their work. When all of the teams have shared, talk as a group about the presentations. Were any events included in all presentations? Were others omitted? Why? What seem to be the most significant events in Elijah's life?

OPTION B

Needed: Bibles, a Bible concordance or Bible dictionary, "Where Is God?" handouts, pencils

Remind the youth that when Elijah was told to look for God, he discovered that God was not in the places that he expected. Invite the participants to work in groups of two to four. Give each group a Bible and a copy of the handout "Where Is God?" Ask the youth to use the handouts to discover stories in Scripture in which people found God in wind, fire, earthquake, and silence. The handout lists suggested Scriptures, but encourage the youth to use Bible study tools to discover other people who met God in these places. Allow five to ten minutes for this activity. When most of the youth have finished, talk together about what they discovered.

Living the Story (5–10 minutes)

OPTION A

Form a circle and invite the participants to close the session by answering the question that God asked Elijah in the story: As you look at yourself in relation to God and others, what are you doing here? Be sure to grant the option of not answering the question if it is too difficult, and allow the youth to frame their understanding of the question in any way they choose.

After everyone has been given a chance to answer, remind the group that after Elijah talked with God, he returned to the world and did things for God. As they leave this session, invite them to consider what their answers to the question might lead them to do. Close with a prayer.

OPTION B
Needed: newsprint, markers, and the following optional equipment—a fan, dominos, blocks, candle, and matches
Hang newsprint on the wall. Turn on the fan, if you brought one, and invite the youth to talk about events or experiences in their lives or in the lives of people they know that are like the wind. For example, these could be times when everything is blowing in different directions. List some of these experiences on the newsprint under the heading "Wind." Next, list experiences that are like an earthquake, events that shake people's foundations. Let a pile of dominos or blocks fall while you make this list. Then light a candle and list experiences that are like fire, such as times that people are very excited about something.

Ask the youth to share which category most closely resembles their lives. Do not force anyone to do this, but do not rush the process either. Wait patiently. Then invite the youth into a time of silence. Encourage them to close their eyes and breathe deeply, trying to relax completely. After a few minutes of silence, ask them to imagine that they hear God asking them the question that God asked Elijah: "What are you doing here?" Invite them to talk with God about this question and to consider how they

will respond. After a few moments of silence, tell the youth that when they are ready, they may leave the room. Ask them to leave quietly so that they do not disturb people who may still be talking with God.

Things to Ponder
Option B under "Living the Story" ends with an open-ended prayer exercise. Some youth appreciate this kind of experience while others struggle to get through it. Those who struggle may be eager to leave as soon as you give them permission to do so. Those who appreciate this experience may welcome the opportunity to debrief it with you. To meet the needs of both groups, try to station yourself at the door to be available to youth as they leave. Invite those who stay longer to talk about what they were thinking and feeling during this exercise.

Looking Ahead
The next session looks at the walk to Emmaus from Luke 24:13–35. In keeping with that theme, some options in the session involve walking about. Should you choose those options, it's important that you prepare your walking place and route in advance. Alert the participants to wear appropriate shoes and clothes for walking. Also, the preparation for the next session involves posting street signs in the meeting area. If you do not have access to any, you might want to make them in advance.

~~~~~~

Elijah and Me

We all have our problems, and the more we think about them, the more we find that everyone's problems are pretty similar. In the space below, we have listed some of Elijah's problems. Your job is to show where you have had to contend with similar problems. Feel free to add a few issues to the list if you need to.

Elijah	Me
■ He didn't make friends easily.	■
■ Powerful people didn't like him.	■
■ He was confused about his role in life.	■
■ His religion was unpopular.	■
■ He was often frightened.	■
■ Some people thought he was weird.	■
■ He was very often alone.	■
■ He didn't play well with the rest of the kids.	■
■ He was very argumentative.	■

Your own observations about Elijah:

■

■

■

■

■

Where Is God?

Elijah is told to be on the lookout for God, so Elijah looks in the usual places—wind, earthquake, and fire. Look up some of the passages listed below, or find others by looking up these words in a biblical concordance or Bible dictionary. Who found God in those places? Why did Elijah look there? Where did Elijah finally find God?

Wind
Genesis 8:1

Earthquake
Psalm 114

Fire
Exodus 3:1–7

Silence
1 Kings 19:11–13

3. Jesus Himself Came Near

Bible Story: Luke 24:13–35

A Story behind the Story

The story of Jesus' appearance on the road to Emmaus takes place on the day of the Resurrection. Earlier that day, the women discovered that Jesus' tomb was empty. Two dazzling messengers explained that Jesus had risen. The women told the apostles this good news, but the apostles did not believe them. Only Simon Peter returned to the tomb and saw what the women saw.

On this same day, Luke explains, two others were traveling from Jerusalem to Emmaus, talking together about the events of the previous week. Suddenly, Jesus came near, but they did not realize who he was. Jesus stayed with them, veiled by anonymity, until the end of the day. In the course of this day, these unsuspecting travelers became aware of the presence of Jesus in three ways.

Their first awareness came through Scripture. The travelers outlined the events of the week to Jesus, but they did not understand their significance. Jesus used the Hebrew Scriptures to explain the meaning of these events to them (Luke 24:27).

The second revelation took place at the table. The weary travelers stopped to rest for the evening and invited Jesus to stay with them. They shared a meal, and during the meal Jesus "took bread, blessed and broke it, and gave it to them" (Luke 24:30). This language mirrors the language used to describe Jesus' last supper with his disciples (Luke 22:19) and the feeding of the five thousand (Luke 9:16). Because Jesus was present with them, this common meal became a holy moment. "Their eyes were opened, and they recognized him" (Luke 24:31). As soon as they recognized him, he vanished from their physical sight.

The third moment of insight came with the community of believers. The two hurried back to Jerusalem to tell the eleven apostles and other followers of Jesus what they had seen and experienced. There they heard that Jesus had also appeared to Simon. While they were discussing these things, Jesus appeared again in the company of the believers (Luke 24:36 and following.) Though these verses are not part of the session for today, they still remind us that Christ is present with his gathered people.

May Christ be present with your group as you encounter this story in Scripture, recall meals around Christ's table, and share in fellowship together.

Enter the Story

Find a time and place where you can read the story and consider it. Bring writing material. Read the story, making note of questions and observations as you proceed. Read the story again and consider how your own story is related to this ancient story. Make some notes of these thoughts too.

Take a moment to remember those times when you were traveling and had a very meaningful experience. What was it that made the experience so memorable? How can you help the youth find meaning in

POSSIBLE YOUTH CONTACT POINTS

- Where am I going with my life?
- At what points in my life do I encounter Jesus?
- How do I recognize God when God intervenes in my life?
- How does my choice of traveling companions affect my journey?
- In what ways can I be a good companion to others on their life journeys?
- Is Jesus really present in my life, or do I travel alone?

YOU MAY NEED

- road signs or traffic symbols (optional)
- construction paper and scissors
- small suitcase (optional)
- small Bible or copy of Luke 24:13–35
- paper and pencils
- tape
- markers
- newsprint
- large sheets of paper folded like maps
- Bible study materials (concordance, dictionary, commentaries)
- "Breaking Bread" handouts
- "Meeting God" handouts
- sliced loaf of bread
- scrap paper

their experiences? Where is God in the more moving experiences in our lives, and how do we recognize God's presence there?

Pray for the youth and for yourself as you prepare to encounter this story of journey together.

Setting the Stage (10 minutes)

Needed: a collection of road signs (optional), construction paper, scissors

If you wish, decorate your meeting space with road signs, traffic symbols, destination markers, and other signs that remind you of traveling by road. Check in with youth as they arrive. What's new? Have any significant events taken place in their lives since your last meeting? If you plan to use Option A under "Reacting to the Story," invite youth to make footprints during this time. Work in groups to trace around their shoes on construction paper and cut out footprints. Save these for later.

OPTION A

Needed: small suitcase (optional)

As you get ready to consider today's story from the Bible, ask for volunteers to share a story about something important that happened to them on a trip. If you have a small suitcase, give it to the youth who is speaking to hold while he or she tells about what happened on the trip. When the youth finishes speaking, pass the suitcase to the next volunteer. Encourage the participants to talk about where they were going, what happened, what the ultimate consequences of the incident were, what they learned from

it, and other factors that made the trip memorable. If there are too few volunteers to make this activity work, encourage a few of the youth to talk about memorable trips from history, popular movies, television shows, or trips the youth have taken together. Following the stories, invite others in the group to ask questions or check observations with the storyteller.

OPTION B

Play "I'm Going on a Trip." Begin by forming a circle and saying, "I'm going on a trip, and I'm taking X." Identify the item that you are taking. The person to your right then says, "I'm going on a trip, and I'm taking X and Y." This person repeats the item that you mentioned and adds another to the list. The next person to the right says, "I'm going on a trip, and I'm taking X and Y and Z." Keep playing in this way, with each person repeating all the items on the list in their proper order and adding one more until someone forgets an item.

Telling the Story (10–15 minutes)

OPTION A

Needed: a small Bible or a photocopy of Luke 24:13–35

Tell the group that today's story is about a walk that some followers of Jesus took soon after he died on the cross. Explain that some women who were friends of Jesus went to the tomb but his body was not there. Organize everyone to go on a walk with you, then set out walking, either inside the building or outside, weather permitting. You have two options for telling the story. One is to encourage the members of the group to cluster close by you as you walk, and read or tell the story while you are walking. If you choose this option, be sure that your walking and storytelling will not disrupt other groups that may be nearby. Another option is to walk to a specified place quietly, and when you arrive there, read or tell Luke 24:13–35 to the group as clearly as possible. After telling the story, you may either return to your meeting place or stay where you are while you react to the story.

OPTION B

Needed: paper, pencils, Bible
Distribute writing materials to the youth and tell them that you are about to read an important story about some people who were on a journey. Say that in order to get the most out of the story they will need to pay careful attention to what is happening on the way. Invite them each to list on their papers one word that they expect to hear as the story is read. If someone has a hard time choosing a word, offer some suggestions from an experience typical of taking a journey. What do the youth expect to be part of a journey experience? As you read the story, the youth should count the number of times you say their words and mark the numbers on their sheets of paper.

After making sure that everyone understands the instructions and has written a word, explain that this story takes place soon after Jesus rose from the dead. News of the empty tomb is just beginning to spread among followers of Jesus. Read Luke 24:13–35 as carefully

and clearly as possible. Pause for a second or two at the end of each sentence to allow youth time to adequately process the words as you read them.

Reacting to the Story (10 minutes)

OPTION A

If you chose Option A under "Telling the Story," you may want to use the following exercise for this segment.
Needed: footprints made at the beginning of the session, markers, tape
Invite the youth to form groups of two or three. Ask the groups to walk together around your meeting space and try to recall the story together. What characters are present in the story? What happened first, next, and so on? If your meeting space is not large enough to allow youth to walk during this activity, consider doing this part of the activity outside or in a larger space. Tell the groups to sit down when they feel that they have remembered most of the story. Allow no more than five minutes for remembering the story.

When most of the groups are seated, return to your meeting area, if you are not already there, and gather around a table. Distribute the footprints that the youth made at the beginning of the session. Ask for a volunteer to tell you what the first part of the story was. Invite someone to write that on one of the footprints and tape that footprint to the wall. Do the same with the other parts of the story until you have recalled the entire story. When all of the footprints are on the wall, review the order of events to see if you recalled the story correctly. Then invite the youth to write their names on the footprint containing the part of the story that is most meaningful to them.

OPTION B
If you chose Option B under "Telling the Story" above, you may want to use the following exercise for this segment.
Needed: markers, newsprint
Invite volunteers to share their words and the number of times they occurred with the rest of the group. As each one shares, have a volunteer list the results on newsprint. After everyone is finished, discuss the findings by asking questions like the following:
■ What words appeared most often on your papers and why?
■ What other words might you have expected to see and why?
■ How is this activity like what was going on in the story?

Connecting to the Story (10–15 minutes)
OPTION A
Needed: large sheets of paper (possibly folded like road maps), markers, pencils
Distribute writing materials and ask the youth to draw road maps of their lives marking major events that have happened to them along the way. Invite them to include common events like birth, education, and the births of siblings as well as difficult events like the death of a relative, parents' divorce, or a move. Ask the youth to think about times in their lives when they have

known that Jesus was walking with them. Have them mark those places with a cross. Allow about five minutes for the youth to complete their life maps.

When most have finished, ask the youth to form groups of two or three and take turns sharing their life maps, describing the key events in their lives and times along the way when they knew that Jesus was walking with them. After each person has shared, invite group members to take turns looking at their partners' maps and pointing out places where Jesus may have been with them, even though they did not recognize it at the time. Have them mark these places with a cross as well.

Talk together about this activity. Ask questions such as:
■ Were other people able to identify Jesus' presence even when we could not?
■ Why is this the case?
■ How does this activity relate to the story we are encountering today?

OPTION B
Needed: pencils, paper, newsprint, markers
Invite the youth to think about their lives as a road trip. Who are their chief traveling companions? Ask them to list on the paper all of the people who are traveling with them and to write beside each name a brief description of how this person helps them along the way. Remind the youth to include Jesus on their lists. Allow about five minutes for youth to complete their lists. Invite them to share their lists out loud.

As they do so, make a large composite list. Rather than include individual names on the composite list, write things like "parents," "teachers," "friends," and so on. After completing this list, talk together about the different ways that Jesus helps us along our way.

Exploring the Story
(10–15 minutes)
OPTION A
Needed: Bibles, Bible concordance, pencils, "Breaking Bread" handouts
Distribute pencils and "Breaking Bread" handouts and encourage everyone to read and work through the handout. Allow the youth to work in groups if they wish. Encourage them to look up the word *bread* in a concordance to find other places in Scripture where it is mentioned.

After about ten minutes, or when most of the youth appear to have finished their work, gather the group and invite volunteers to share their findings with the rest of the group. Then talk together about some of the following questions:
■ What stories in the Bible other than the ones listed on the handout deal with bread?
■ What is the significance of bread in the Bible?
■ Why do you think that Jesus became known to the people on the road to Emmaus in the breaking of the bread?
■ What does this suggest about our own worship?
■ How do we use bread?
■ How is Jesus known to us when we eat bread?

OPTION B
Needed: Bibles, reference materials, pencils, "Meeting God" handouts, a large piece of newsprint, markers
Form teams of two or three and give each team pencils, at least one copy of the "Meeting God" handout, and a Bible. Invite the teams to work through the handout together, writing their observations on the handout as they work. If reference materials are available, make sure that they are shared equally among the teams.

After about ten minutes, or when most of the teams appear to have completed their work, call time, gather the group, and invite representatives from each team to read aloud their team's findings as you or a volunteer write them on newsprint. When duplicate items are read, indicate them with check marks next to the item on the newsprint. After all of the findings have been shared, discuss them with the group, using the following questions:
■ What do these stories have in common?
■ Were the characters in the stories looking for God, or were they surprised by God?
■ What do their findings say about the nature of meeting God?
■ In what ways does God come to us?

Living the Story
(5 minutes)
OPTION A
Needed: a sliced loaf of bread, the more ordinary the better
Form a circle and tell the group that the story they explored in this

session is about people who met Jesus while they were traveling somewhere. Remind the group that they, too, are traveling a road to somewhere. They may not know where they are going or where the road will lead, but they are all on a life journey.

Ask for volunteers to talk about things that are needed on their life journey. These may include companionship, shelter, support from others, education, and so on. End this discussion by reminding the group that one of their most basic needs for this journey is food, or bread. Remind the youth that when the travelers to Emmaus stopped for a meal, they recognized who Jesus was.

Take out the loaf of sliced bread. Invite the youth to pass the loaf around the circle. Ask that as each person receives the loaf, he or she take a slice of bread and give the loaf to the person to the right, saying "Jesus be with you wherever you go." When everyone has received a slice of bread, invite the youth to eat the bread in silence and offer silent prayers to God.

OPTION B
Needed: scrap paper and pencils
Form a circle and distribute the writing materials. Tell the group that the story you have explored for this session is one in which people met with Jesus while they were on their way somewhere. Ask the youth to look toward their possible future and think of one place they might meet Jesus on their way. This can be a location, a stage in life, an event, or something symbolic. Encourage the members of the group to write that anticipated meeting spot on

their paper and put it away for their own future reference.

After a couple of minutes, or when everyone appears to have finished, ask for some volunteers to share their thoughts about what they have written. Encourage youth to ask any questions they might have as these things are shared. Upon the completion of this sharing, close with a group prayer that you may all be prepared to meet Jesus when he visits.

Things to Ponder
Adolescence is a time in which people are concerned about the future but often have no sense of where they are heading. Youth frequently feel isolated and lonely. It can be hard for teens to realize that someone is walking with them. Many may have difficulty with the segments of this session that ask them to take stock of this issue. Watch closely to see whether these activities are producing despair or hope, and be prepared to emphasize hope. In some cases, the knowledge that we are not alone can make the difference between life and death for a teenager.

Looking Ahead
Option A of "Setting the Stage" in the next session asks you to display the front pages of sensational tabloid newspapers in the room. If you plan to use this option, purchase a few of these papers ahead of time. Try to find a paper with headlines that are appropriate to your setting and the maturity level of your group. A word to the wise: bring front pages only. The youth may become distracted by the stories printed inside.

~~~~~~~

Breaking Bread

Bread may be common and boring to us, but it is a big deal in the Bible. Amazing things happen when people eat bread. Look up some of the stories mentioned here, or find other places in the Bible where bread is mentioned. What happened when people ate bread?

Exodus 16:3–15

1 Kings 17:8–16

Matthew 6:11

Matthew 14:13–21

Mark 14:22

John 6:30–35

Meeting God

Today we go in search of people who met God. In the space below, list as many accounts of people meeting God as you can find or remember, telling who they were, where they met God, and the Scripture reference for the meeting (if you can track it down). We've already given you one, so the rest should be easy. Happy hunting!

Who?	Where?	Scripture?
Adam	Garden of Eden	Genesis 2–3

4. Unless I See

Bible Story: John 20:19–29

A Story behind the Story

The story of "Doubting Thomas" is one of the more well-known accounts of the resurrected Christ appearing to the disciples. For reasons that are not clearly explained in John's Gospel, Thomas was not present when Jesus first appeared to his followers following the resurrection. This resurrection appearance was amazing in itself—Jesus came to the disciples when they were hiding behind locked doors. No wonder Thomas could not believe it! The other disciples shared the good news with Thomas, saying, "We have seen the Lord," but Thomas refused to believe unless he saw the risen Lord himself. Because of his reluctance to believe everything he heard, Thomas is remembered as a doubter and often ridiculed for his lack of faith.

But perhaps this description of Thomas is not fair, for Thomas certainly was not alone in his questions. Thomas serves an important function in John's account of Jesus' resurrection. Like Thomas, readers of John's Gospel (both when it was first written and now) were not present when Jesus arose from the grave. They did not see the first resurrection appearance with their own eyes. Through Thomas, who is undoubtedly voicing misgivings felt by the reader, the reader is invited to touch the scars of crucifixion and remove any doubt that Christ arose. Rather than looking down on Thomas as a person of weak faith, perhaps we should recognize that he was the only person among the disciples whose faith was strong enough to voice misgivings. By voicing his own doubts, he allows us all to touch Christ.

This story is important in John's Gospel for other reasons as well. First, John uses this story to establish the reality of Jesus' resurrection. This passage makes clear in a physical way that Jesus has returned from the grave. Moreover, when Thomas recognizes Jesus as "my Lord and my God," we hear a decisive and final summation of who and what Jesus is. The "blessing" that follows this statement is arguably the point of the entire gospel. Jesus is the Lord and God both of those who see and believe and of those who do not see and still believe. Future disciples who do not see the risen Christ in physical form and yet believe in him are declared blessed.

Enter the Story

Find a time and place where you can read the story and consider it. Bring writing materials. Read John 20:19–29, making notes of any questions or observations you might have. Read the story again and consider how your own story is related to this ancient story. How have you traditionally interpreted this story? How do you feel about Thomas and the concerns he raises? Do you sympathize with him, or do you look down on him for not believing immediately? Make notes of your thoughts.

Take a moment to remember some of the dubious situations in which you've found yourself. How do you deal with the uncertainty? How do you express doubts and questions? Think about the youth

- Do I believe everything I have heard about Jesus?
- Is it okay to have doubts?
- Is it appropriate to express my doubts?
- What good can come from skepticism?
- In what ways is the Resurrection real for me?
- What do I believe about Jesus?

YOU MAY NEED

- tabloid newspapers
- blank paper and markers
- notepads and pencils for youth
- different translations of Scripture
- Bibles
- paper and pencils
- "Opinion Page" handouts
- Bible study resources (commentaries, concordance, dictionary, encyclopedia)
- "Doubting Thomas?" handouts
- olive oil in two small bowls

in your group. With what doubts do they struggle? What questions do they have? Are they comfortable with sharing their doubts, or do they feel a need to hide their questions?

Pray and think deeply about the significance of this story before you go to help others experience it.

Setting the Stage (10 minutes)
OPTION A
Needed: front pages from tabloids and other sensationalistic newspapers, blank paper, markers
Before the session begins, make a collection of tabloid newspapers and post the front pages on the walls of the meeting space. Hang blank sheets of paper on the walls as well. As youth arrive, invite them to make up their own sensationalistic headlines and write them on the blank sheets. (Examples: "The Amazing Bigfoot Diet" or "Scientists Discover Candy Bar on Mars.")

When most of the youth are present, form two or more teams of two to five players. Give each group paper and markers. Ask the groups to make up headlines describing amazing activities that they could do together as a group. These headlines could describe exaggerated versions of actual events (example: "Teens Imprisoned in Church Building" as a headline for a youth lock-in) or events that never took place (example: "Youth Return from Mission Trip to Mars"). Allow a few minutes for teams to make up headlines. Then invite the teams to take turns sharing headlines with the larger group. After each headline, ask the other

youth to decide whether it exaggerates an actual event or describes a totally false event.

Introduce the story from John 20:19–29 by saying that it describes an event experienced by a group of Jesus' followers that was hard for one member of the group to believe.

OPTION B
Needed: newsprint and markers
As youth arrive, invite them to arrange your meeting space to look like a "hideout." You might use some of the usual trappings of a hideout (bad furniture, dim light, spooky atmosphere, and so on). Just for fun, place a sign out front that says something like "Youth group hideout. Do not look for us here."

Hang three sheets of newsprint on the wall. Select a volunteer to write on one piece of newsprint, "Who hangs out in a hideout like this?" on another, "Why do people hide?" and on the third, "What happens when someone shows up in a hideout unexpectedly?" Gather the group around the newsprint and invite them to answer these questions together. Encourage any answers the youth may wish to give, and have the volunteer write them on the newsprint as they are called out.

Introduce the story by telling the group that it describes a time when a group of Jesus' followers were hiding out and an unexpected visitor showed up.

Telling the Story (10–15 minutes)
OPTION A
If you chose Option A under "Setting the Stage" above, you

*may want to use the following
exercise for this segment.*
***Needed: notepads and pencils
for each youth, several different
translations of the Bible***
Give notepads and pencils to youth
and invite them to pretend that they
are reporters who have gathered
for a press conference. (If you have
time, set up chairs in rows and
stand in front of the group, as if
you were leading a real press conference.) Tell the group that rumors
are circulating that Jesus of
Nazareth has risen from the dead.
Some of his followers have seen him
and even touched his wounds. One
of his followers prepared a statement describing the event, and you
will read the statement to them.
Encourage the "reporters" to take
notes as they listen to you read John
20:19–29. Read the passage slowly
and carefully without taking questions from the "reporters." After
you finish the first reading, explain
that the statement was originally
written in Greek and ask the
"reporters" if they would like
you to read another translation
of the statement. If so, read John
20:19–29 from another translation,
again without taking questions.

OPTION B
*If you chose Option B under
"Setting the Stage" above, you
may want to use the following
exercise for this segment.*
Needed: Bibles
Invite the group to imagine that
they are followers of Jesus hiding
out in this place after his death.
Talk together about why they might
be afraid or why they might need
to hide. Distribute Bibles and help

everyone find John 20:19–29. Then
ask for one volunteer to play the
part of Jesus and another to play
the part of Thomas. Send these
people out of the room with their
Bibles, and ask them to stay close
enough to the hideout to hear what
is happening. Invite a volunteer to
begin reading John 20:19–29, pausing when necessary to set up the
scenes. Bring Jesus into the room
after reading verse 19. Send the
other disciples out to find Thomas
after reading verse 25.

Reacting to the Story
(10 minutes)
OPTION A
*If you chose Option A under
"Telling the Story" above, you
may want to use the following
exercise for this segment.*
Needed: newsprint, markers, paper
After reading the story, invite the
"reporters" to ask questions. Try
to answer them on the basis of this
text alone. Reread portions of the
passage if necessary. If the text does
not provide an answer for a particular question, tell them that you
do not have that information at this
time. After they have asked all of
the questions that can be answered
by this text, ask them to list other
questions that they have. Write
these on newsprint so that everyone
can see. Talk together about how
they might find answers to these
questions. Whom would they like
to interview? What questions would
they ask? What sort of research
might they do? Where would they
begin their research?

Form pairs and give each pair
paper and a marker. Ask each pair
to develop a headline for this story

that summarizes what happened. When pairs have finished their work, invite them to share their headlines with the large group.

OPTION B
Needed: paper, pencils, Bibles
Form three groups. Give each group paper, a pencil, and a Bible. Ask one group to think of questions they would like to ask Thomas on the basis of this story. Ask the second group to think of questions they would like to ask Jesus, and the third to think of questions they would like to ask the other disciples. Allow three to five minutes for groups to work. Then pass the lists of questions to the other groups, allowing each group to add questions that they would like to ask Thomas, Jesus, or the other disciples. When all three groups have added questions to all three lists, read the three lists aloud. Then compare the lists by asking the youth to decide which character or group of characters prompted the most questions, which prompted the most unusual question, and which prompted the most crucial question.

Connecting to the Story (10–15 minutes)
OPTION A
If you chose Option A under "Reacting to the Story" above, you may want to use the following exercise for this segment.
Needed: Bibles, pencils, "Opinion Page" handouts
Give each youth a copy of the "Opinion Page" handout and a Bible. Explain that journalists usually try to present the facts of a story without offering their personal

opinions about the story. When they wish to offer a personal opinion or to convince others to believe what they believe, they write an editorial. This handout invites the youth to write a personal editorial explaining what they believe about the resurrection of Jesus. The handout provides an outline for the editorial, but the youth do not have to follow it. They may organize the editorials as they wish. Invite them to use their Bibles to find information to include in their editorials. Encourage them to work quietly and to allow each person to express his or her own opinions.

After about ten minutes, or when most youth appear to have completed their work, call time. Gather the group and invite volunteers to share what they have written. Talk together about the following questions:
■ What do the editorials have in common?
■ How do they differ?
■ What do we believe about Jesus' resurrection?
■ Why do we believe it?

OPTION B
If you used Option B under "Reacting to the Story" above, you may want to use the following exercise for this segment.
Needed: pencils and paper
Invite the youth to form groups of four to eight. Tell them that just as we have questions about this passage that we would like to ask Jesus, Thomas, or the other disciples, many people have questions about the resurrection of Jesus that they would like to ask. Allow three to five minutes for the youth to

work in groups to list some of these questions. These could be questions that they have asked, questions that they would like to ask, or questions that other people they know have asked. Tell the youth that it is okay to ask any question in this activity. After the groups have completed their lists, talk together about the questions they posed. Ask the participants to suggest who might be able to respond effectively to the questions. List these individuals beside the questions.

**Exploring the Story
(10–15 minutes)**
OPTION A
Needed: Bible concordance, commentaries, dictionaries, or encyclopedias, "Doubting Thomas?" handouts
Invite youth to learn more about Thomas. Form small groups of two or more youth and give each group a different kind of Bible study aid. For example, give one group a concordance, one a commentary, one a dictionary, and so on. Ask each group to look up information about Thomas in their resource and prepare to share what they find with the rest of the group. After groups have shared their findings, give each youth a copy of the "Doubting Thomas?" handout and a pencil. Ask the youth if they have ever heard of "Doubting Thomas." Ask whether, given what they have now learned about Thomas, they feel that is an appropriate name for him. Invite those who wish to do so to choose a new name for Thomas. Talk together about the names they chose and why they feel these are more appropriate.

OPTION B
Needed: Bibles, pencils and paper, newsprint, markers
Form four teams and give each team paper, pencils, and a Bible. Assign each team one of the versions of the Easter story: Matthew 28, Mark 16, Luke 24, or John 20–21. Ask the participants to pay special attention to the resurrection appearances of Jesus found in their version of the story. Allow time for the teams to read the story and to list all of the people mentioned who saw Jesus after he rose from the dead. When the teams finish their research, ask them to share their findings with the larger group. Post newsprint on the wall and make a composite list of everyone who saw Jesus after he arose from the dead.

As a group, talk together about the following questions:
■ Which version of the Easter story seems most unusual? Why?
■ How do the stories differ?
■ How are they the same?
■ Which version surprised you the most? Why?
■ How does this activity affect your understanding of the resurrection of Jesus?
■ What do you believe about Jesus' resurrection?

**Living the Story
(5 minutes)**
OPTION A
Close by reminding the youth that Thomas is often remembered as "Doubting Thomas." That is probably not the way he would have wanted to be remembered, and the youth may have decided that that is not a fair description of his faith in Christ. Ask the youth to consider

how they want people to remember their faith. What name do they want others to give to them? Invite youth who are willing to share this name with the rest of the group. Close with prayer, thanking God for Thomas's example and asking God to help us to be faithful as we ask questions and seek to follow Jesus.

OPTION B

Needed: Olive oil in a small bowl

Form a circle and tell the group that a sense of mystery is one of the hallmarks of their Christian heritage. There is much about God that we will never be able to understand. One way in which Christians have traditionally dealt with their uncertainty is through rituals that explore and express the sense of mystery in which they are participating.

Continue by telling the youth that oil is one of the tools used in the more ancient rituals of our faith. As a practical means of "anointing" someone, people would touch the tip of their thumb to some oil, then dab it lightly on another person's forehead. Demonstrate on a volunteer, and then invite the group to share in the experience by passing a small bowl with oil around the circle. Instruct the youth to say, as they dab the oil on the forehead of the person next to them, "Blessed are those who have not seen, but have come to believe."

When the circle has been completed and the bowls set aside, explain to the group that the oil should serve as a reminder that they have been touched by one who is exploring the same mysteries that they are exploring. Close with a prayer that the participants might feel God's presence as they deepen their faith and deal with the uncertainties of the world around them.

Things to Ponder

Some teenagers embrace doubt and uncertainty, while others view these questions as frightening threats to faith. You may have people in your group who identify with Thomas and ask the same questions that he asked, and you may have people who criticize him for his questions. If possible, try to create an atmosphere where both groups of youth can feel comfortable. Encourage the doubters to listen carefully to the beliefs of those who do not question. Encourage those who do not doubt to respect the questions asked by those who do.

Looking Ahead

The next session focuses on the murder of Abel in Genesis 4. One of the options in "Telling the Story" suggests inviting someone to read the passage as a one-person show using different voices for the different characters in the story. Consider asking a youth with dramatic talent to prepare to do this for the next session. Several of the options use a trial motif to discuss what Cain did and how the youth feel about his punishment. You might take a few minutes to watch a courtroom drama on television. This will help you prepare for the procedures of the mock trial.

30

OPINION PAGE

Did Jesus rise from the dead?

Jesus of Nazareth was crucified like a criminal and buried in a tomb. Yet, many of his followers report that they have seen him and that he is alive.

I am especially intrigued
by the report found in . . .

This is what I believe:

What does this mean
for us?

I encourage other people who may struggle
with this belief to . . .

Doubting Thomas?

Poor Thomas. He made one honest statement, and now he is ridiculed as "Doubting Thomas." Do you think that name fits? What other words might describe him? Choose one of these or come up with your own name for him.

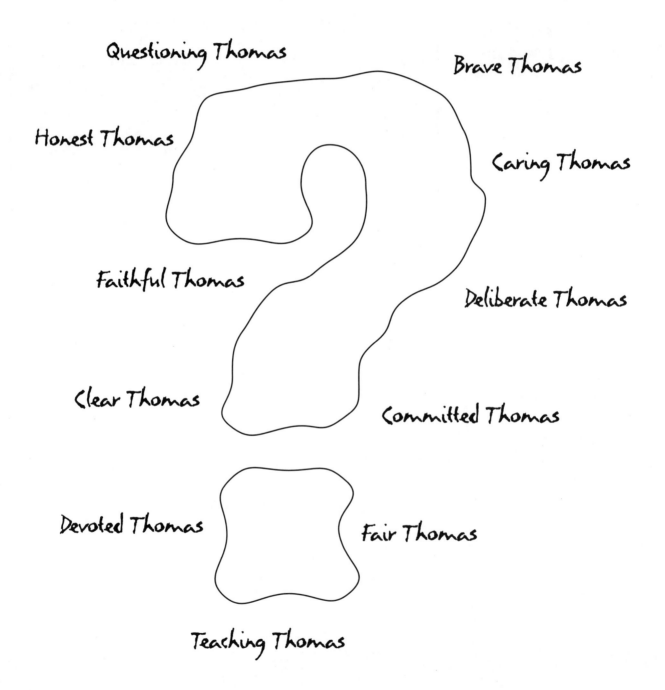

Questioning Thomas

Brave Thomas

Honest Thomas

Caring Thomas

Faithful Thomas

Deliberate Thomas

Clear Thomas

Committed Thomas

Devoted Thomas

Fair Thomas

Teaching Thomas

5. Where Is Your Brother?

Bible Story: Genesis 4:1–16

Section Two

Covenant

by Steven B. Lawrence

A Story behind the Story

The story of Cain and Abel is part of the opening chapters of Genesis, a portion referred to as primeval history. The stories recorded in Genesis chapters 1–11 are told more for their theological importance than for their scientific or historical meaning. For this reason, these stories do not include the answers to many of the questions we really want to ask. For example: If there are only four people, why is Cain worried about being killed? Whom does Cain marry? What was wrong with Cain's offering? Questions like these can drive us to create elaborate guesses and suppositions to get answers. Sometimes these "answers" take us far away from the main point of the story. As tempting as it is to pursue these questions, focus instead on the details that are observable in the text.

Primeval history is concerned with the origin of things, how things came to be. So in addition to our questions about who, what, where, and when, we must also be sure to ask why. Why was this story told? What is its significance? What was the point of recording it? We shift from looking at what was said to what was meant. Cain and Abel were brothers, born a generation after the Fall. Sin has moved from disobedience and deceit to envy and murder.

Genesis chapter 4 begins like a story about a family. Soon, however, Adam, Eve, and Abel drop away and Cain emerges as the dominant character. The name Cain means "productive" (Genesis 4:1); the name Abel means, "vapor, nothingness." As strange as it sounds, Abel is less than a full actor in this drama. He is silent throughout (until his blood cries out to God, verse 10). As much as we may want to identify with Abel as the victim, Cain's thoughts and actions are the reason this story was preserved and told. We have to identify with the "bad guy" in the text. We have to understand him. We do not have to explain or justify his feelings and actions, but we do have to examine them. That could be uncomfortable because it will unveil the similarities between Cain and us.[1]

Enter the Story

As you read the story, think of a time you felt angry or sad and you directed that emotion at someone who was completely disconnected from the situation that was upsetting you. You may want to do some writing or make a journal entry recounting such an experience. Include details like: What was the real issue? Who was the innocent bystander who got caught in the middle? What or who helped you to see your error? Imagine what might have happened if Cain had taken a moment to step back from his situation and look at it through calmer eyes. As you prepare this lesson, consider that many of our conflicts with others

POSSIBLE YOUTH CONTACT POINTS

- How well do I get along with my siblings?
- How are responsibilities in the family based on birth order?
- How can I do better if I don't know what I did wrong?
- Am I my brother's (or sister's) keeper?
- Who are my brothers and sisters?

YOU MAY NEED

- name tags
- Bibles
- newsprint, markers
- judge's robe and gavel (optional)
- "Turning Up the Heat" handouts
- "Perspectives" handouts
- Bible study aids (commentaries, study Bibles)
- writing paper
- envelopes
- stamps

are a working out of struggles from within.

Cain had certain responsibilities and expectations because he was the firstborn. Research and anecdotal information about the differences in people because of birth order are available on the Internet. Lorie M. Sutter, on the Ohio State University website, says firstborns are generally high achievers, perfectionists, organized, rule keepers, and detail people.[2] Does that sound like Cain? Does it shed light on his reactions in the story?

Setting the Stage (5 minutes)
OPTION A
Needed: name tags
As the youth arrive, invite them to create name tags for themselves that identify their birth order. You can use preprinted name tags or make them from construction paper. Ask participants to write their names and one these birth order designations: Only Child, Firstborn (Oldest), Middle-Born, Last-Born (Youngest.) When the name tags are complete, have each person share just his or her name and birth order designation. Be prepared for the possibility that some learners may come from blended families. You may ask youth to use the birth order in their family of origin or in the family with whom they spend most of their time. After all have shared, ask the youth to say their names again and this time be more detailed about their birth order status by adding details like gender (First Girl), total number

of siblings, blended family, and so on. Ask participants with similar descriptions to sit together during the "Telling the Story" portion of the session.

OPTION B
Talk with the youth as they enter the room. When most have arrived, ask each youth to answer this question briefly: "When you were younger, what did you get busted for that your younger siblings or cousins got away with?" Talk together about this question and try to make the conversation light and fun. Then invite the learners, as they listen to the Scripture, to think about how siblings get along.

Telling the Story (5–10 minutes)
OPTION A
Needed: Bibles
Before reading the story, form groups of youth based on birth order. (If you chose Option A in "Setting the Stage," you've already done this.) Place firstborns in one group, youngest children in another group, and everyone else in a third group. Distribute Bibles and help everyone find Genesis 4:1–16. Ask the firstborns to listen and notice what Cain says and does. Ask the youngest children to listen and notice what Abel says and does. Ask the other youth to listen and notice what God says and does. Read the passage aloud. After reading, ask the firstborns to talk about what Cain said and did in the passage. Then talk about what God said and did. Finally, talk about what Abel said and did.

OPTION B
Needed: someone to read the story in a dramatic way
Invite a youth to read Genesis 4:1–16 as a one-person show. If you prefer, you may contact someone prior to the session and ask him or her to prepare this presentation of Scripture, or you may choose to call on an outgoing volunteer or read it yourself. Whoever reads the Scripture should use a different voice for each character and the narrator, or stand in different places to indicate different voices, making a big, dramatic production out of the reading. Ask the reader to take a bow at the end of the show and invite everyone to applaud.

Reacting to the Story (10 to 15 minutes)
OPTION A
Needed: newsprint, markers
Ask the learners to imagine that Cain has been arrested. Work as a large group or form small groups of three to five and talk about the following questions: What do they expect the charge to be? (What did Cain do wrong?) How should Cain plead his case?

Invite the youth to share their responses to these questions. Then write on the board or post a prepared sheet of newsprint with the following options and ask the group to decide how to charge Cain with this murder.
1. Murder One: Premeditated murder
2. Murder Two: Murder committed in the heat of the moment
3. Felony murder: Murder committed in the process of a felony act
4. Involuntary manslaughter: Murder committed by accident
5. Self-defense: Death occurred in the process of defending oneself

When the group has selected a charge, continue with a trial in Option A of "Connecting to the Story."

OPTION B
Needed: newsprint or chalkboard, markers or chalk
Tell the group that this story is filled with many different emotions. Some are clear and obvious while others may be hidden beneath the surface. Invite the learners to identify feelings and emotions that were present in the story. On the newsprint or chalkboard, make a list of these feelings or emotions. After completing the list, go back to each word and ask the youth who it was who experienced that feeling in the story. Write each name next to the corresponding emotion. Talk together about how each person in the story dealt with his or her emotions.

Connecting to the Story (10–15 minutes)
OPTION A
If you chose Option A in "Reacting to the Story" above, you may want to use the following exercise for this segment.
Needed: robe and gavel for a judge (optional)
Form two groups. One will be the prosecution and will need to decide how to convince a jury that Cain is guilty of the charge that was determined in "Reacting to the Story." The other group will be members of the defense team. They will need to

decide how to defend Cain and how to convince a jury that he is not guilty. Allow a few minutes for each team to prepare for the trial. Then hold a brief mock trial and allow each team to make its points and to rebut the statements of the other team. If you wish, you or one of the youth may dress as a judge and keep order during the trial. When the trial is complete, discuss this experience using questions such as these:

■ Which group had the easier job and which had the harder job?
■ What verdict would a jury reach?
■ Was Cain guilty? Of what?
■ What sentence did he deserve?

OPTION B

If you chose Option B in "Reacting to the Story" above, you may want to use the following exercise for this segment.

Needed: "Turning Up the Heat" handouts

Give each youth a copy of the "Turning Up the Heat" handout. This handout presents eight statements that prompt an emotional response. Below each statement are four emotions. There is also one blank space to fill in an additional emotion. Have the youth read the sentences and then draw an arrow to the number that indicates the level of emotion that the statement brings out in them. One (1) represents the emotion inactive, three (3), the emotion in balance, and five (5), the emotion out of control. Have a discussion around the group's responses, using these questions:

■ What things or people "push your buttons"?
■ When do you feel "out of control"?

■ How do you handle strong emotions?

Exploring the Story (10–15 minutes)

OPTION A

Needed: "Perspectives" handouts, Bibles, Bible study aids

There are many ways to read and interpret the story of Cain and Abel, as there are many ways to read and interpret other stories in the Bible. This activity guides youth through the process of thinking about this story from four different points of view. Give each youth a copy of the "Perspectives" handout. Form four groups and ask each group to look at the story from one of the perspectives listed on the handout. If your group is smaller than eight people, form two groups and ask each group to look at two of the perspectives. Allow time for groups to think about the story and discuss the questions on the handout. Then invite them to share what they discovered. Talk together about the following questions:

■ What did you learn in the process of looking at this story in many different ways?
■ Which perspective seems most appropriate to you?
■ What are other possible ways to look at this story?

OPTION B

Needed: Bibles, Bible reference materials such as commentaries and study Bibles

This story probably raises many questions for youth. Ask the group to identify some of these questions. Some of the questions might be:

- Why was God happy with Abel's offering and not happy with Cain's offering?
- Why did Cain kill Abel?
- Why did God allow Abel to be killed?
- What happened to Cain after this?

Write these and any other questions the group might identify in large print on separate pieces of newsprint or large sheets of paper. Place the questions in different parts of the room and invite the youth to go to the question that seems most intriguing to them. Provide Bible study aids such as commentaries and study Bibles, and invite the youth to search for information that pertains to the questions they asked. Allow five to ten minutes for exploring. Then invite the youth to share what they discovered with each other.

Living the Story (5 minutes)
OPTION A
Needed: Stickers or markers
Cain did a horrible thing, and he had to pay a terrible price for his crime. Still, God did not abandon him. Ask the youth to identify things that God did to show that God still cared for Cain. One of these was the mark that God placed on Cain to warn others not to harm him. This was a sign of God's protection and provision. Even though Cain had taken the life of someone else, God still wanted to preserve Cain's life.

Invite the youth to spend a few moments quietly confessing to God some of the mistakes they have made—perhaps times when they lost control and said or did things that hurt others. As they are praying quietly, go to them and place a sticker on their hands or make a small mark on their hands with washable marker. When the prayer time is finished, tell the group that the mark is a sign that God is with them and that God cares for them in spite of the mistakes they have made.

OPTION B
Needed: writing paper, envelopes, stamps, pens
Ask the group to think about things they could do that would heal a family relationship or restore a broken friendship. Give each youth a piece of paper, an envelope, and a pen. Invite them to decide on a course of action and write this down as a promise to themselves in the form of a letter. When they finish writing, ask them to seal their letters and address the letters to themselves. Collect the letters and plan to mail them so that learners receive them thirty days from the day of the session.

Things to Ponder
No matter how Cain's actions are explained, the results are always the same: Abel was dead, and his death did not solve Cain's problems. Cain was still ignorant about the unworthiness of his sacrifice. Further, he had distanced himself from God, the one to whom he wanted to grow closer. Part of growing up is considering the consequences of our actions and learning to choose our next steps wisely. What we think and how we feel are both valuable sources of information.

When we add to them patience, prayer, and the ability to listen, we create the foundation for healthy decision making.

Looking Ahead

The next lesson also asks us to concentrate on a character whose behavior was not exemplary. The story of David and Bathsheba is, on its surface, about adultery and murder and, at its heart, about power and its ability to corrupt. If we keep the story at its surface level, we can condemn the characters and say, "I'd never do that." However, when we acknowledge the seductive lure that power has on us, we may see ourselves in the Scripture.

If you choose Option A under "Telling the Story" in the next session, you may want to make arrangements to have the Bible story from 2 Samuel 11:1–12:7 recorded on audiotape.

Notes

1. Celia Brewer Marshall, *A Guide through the Old Testament* (Louisville, Ky.: Westminster/John Knox Press, 1989), 22.

2. Lorie M. Sutter, Ohio State University Extension Fact Sheet, Family and Consumer Sciences, Birth Order, (http://www.ag.ohio-state.edu/~ohioline/hgy-fact/5000/5279.html).

~~~~~~~~~

Turning Up the Heat

Read each statement and circle the word that describes how you would respond. Then circle the number on the dial that shows how hot that emotion would be in that situation—how much emotion the statement creates in you.

When the things you do are overlooked

Anger   Jealousy   Joy   Satisfaction   _____

When someone else gets credit for something you did

Anger   Jealousy   Joy   Satisfaction   _____

When you give God the best you have

Anger   Jealousy   Joy   Satisfaction   _____

When you make peace between two adversaries

Anger   Jealousy   Joy   Satisfaction   _____

When someone close to you tells a secret he or she promised to keep

Anger   Jealousy   Joy   Satisfaction   _____

When you find out you didn't do as well on an exam as you thought you did

Anger   Jealousy   Joy   Satisfaction   _____

When you discover that others trust you

Anger   Jealousy   Joy   Satisfaction   _____

When someone calls you an insulting name

Anger   Jealousy   Joy   Satisfaction   _____

When you win a prize or and award

Anger   Jealousy   Joy   Satisfaction   _____

When you finally master something that was hard to learn

Anger   Jealousy   Joy   Satisfaction   _____

Perspectives

Some stories in the Bible, like the story of Cain and Abel, contain many levels of meaning. It can be hard to uncover all of these levels at once. You have to dig them up layer by layer. It can help to look at such a story from different perspectives.

Literal history
Assume that this story happened exactly as you read it here.
- What do we learn from this story?
- Why was it recorded?
- What is its message for us?

Allegory
Assume that this story is an allegory. In this type of story, each character represents something else—a group of people, a type of feeling, and so on. Allegories are written to teach complex truths in simple form.
- What might Cain represent?
- What might Abel represent?
- What does the murder of Abel represent?

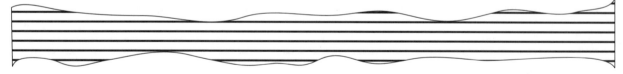

God's story
Assume that this story was written to teach important truths about God.
- What might these truths be?
- What does God want people to learn from this story?

Myth or legend
Pretend that you do not know that this story is from the Bible. Imagine that you found it in a collection of legends like Native American creation stories or the myths of ancient Greece.
- What might this story be about?
- What do you learn by thinking of it in this way?

6. The Thing That David Had Done Displeased the Lord

Bible Story: 2 Samuel 11:1–12:7

A Story behind the Story

Is there a person in the Old Testament better known or celebrated than David? He is famous for his epic battle with the giant Goliath (1 Samuel 17). His musical ability is known through the psalms he authored, and his influence extended to the designing of the temple and royal palace that were eventually built by his son, Solomon. His military victories consolidated the kingdom from "Dan to Beer-sheba" (2 Samuel 3:10), and his reign as Israel's second king erased the shame of Saul and set the foundation for the nation's golden years. The Scriptures say that David's heart was perfect before the Lord (1 Kings 15:3). All of these accomplishments make it difficult to reconcile that picture of David with the one in this passage. This story presents David as an adulterer and murderer.

In light of his fame, one might even wonder how or why this particular story wasn't left out of the collection. Why preserve a story that shames Israel's legendary ruler? The marvelous thing about the Scriptures is that they dare to show human beings with all their strengths and frailties. David's behavior is not excused or covered up. It is written in the pages of the Bible for all to see.

Adultery and murder are the obvious sins in this Scripture passage. They are so prominent that, as we read this story, we can condemn David's behavior and assure ourselves that we would never do such things. On a closer inspection, we may discover other more subtle temptations that do challenge us. For example, David is the king and thus holds the power of life and death over his subjects. Ultimate power is very seductive and often corrupts even the best leaders (Moses, Numbers 20:2–13; Samson, Judges 16:1–20). David also seeks to cover up the wrong he has done. This is a common behavior. If we read carefully and honestly, the story of David and Bathsheba can be not just about some other people who "messed up," but about the struggles we all have to do what is right.

Enter the Story

Many of the issues of the tenth century B.C., the time of David and Bathsheba, are still significant in our own society. Infidelity, murder, conspiracy, and abuse of power all have a contemporary feel, so we can readily identify with the biblical story. In the Bible, these issues may appear to be part of the lives of adults. We know that young people also struggle with these tough topics. Be aware and be open so that they can honestly share their views and their experiences on these subjects.

The reader may find it difficult to suspend judgment on the characters in this story because their faults and strengths seem so obvious. David is

POSSIBLE YOUTH CONTACT POINTS

- **How does power go to your head?**
- **Everyone has a weakness. How do we face ours?**
- **Who will tell us the truth about ourselves?**
- **How do we respond when we discover this truth?**
- **How have I tried to hide from what I have done?**

YOU MAY NEED

- **newsprint and markers or chalkboard and chalk**
- **Bibles**
- **blankets or towels**
- **audio recording of 2 Samuel 11:1–12:7 and a way to play it**
- **paper and pencils**
- **"David Hurt Everybody" handouts**
- **Bible study resources, such as commentaries, on 2 Samuel**
- **"The Life and Times of David the King" handouts**

abusive of his power as king; he can be blamed for everything. Bathsheba is strangely silent throughout the affair. Is she helpless or compliant? Uriah is painfully honest; he draws out our sympathies. Joab is like a loyal lap dog doing the immoral bidding of his king; we hold no sympathy for him. Nathan is the classic prophet—clear and direct; he is the hero. Spend some time "re-humanizing" these characters. As you read, place yourself in their positions and try to see their lives through their eyes.

Setting the Stage (5–10 minutes)

OPTION A

Needed: Newsprint and markers or chalkboard and chalk

Remember the game show "The $10,000 Pyramid"? This activity is that game played in reverse. Announce to the learners that, instead of guessing the category by the examples given, they will start off knowing that the category is "Things That Cannot Be Put Back or Undone." Create on the chalkboard or on newsprint a pyramid made of blocks—three on the bottom row, two on the middle, and one on the top. Write the answers that the youth give in the blocks of the pyramid. Try to get at least six answers. Examples are: When you squeeze too much toothpaste from the tube; when a skydiver jumps from a plane; when you burn the toast. If the game goes quickly, play a second round with the category "Things You Regret." Tell the youth that the story for this session is about someone who did something that could not be undone.

OPTION B

Talk with the youth as they arrive. Invite them to sit in a comfortable place within your meeting area. When most youth have arrived and everyone seems comfortable, ask them to sit in a circle and think about something that they did this week that they wish they could undo or do over again. Invite those who are willing to share, but do not force anyone. When everyone who is willing to offer examples has done so, ask them to explain why they would make different choices now. What happened? What have they learned? What do they know now that they did not know before? Invite them to listen to a story about someone who did something he wished he could undo.

Telling the Story (5–10 minutes)

OPTION A

Needed: Audio recording of 2 Samuel 11:1–12:7, CD or tape player, paper and pencils

Prior to the session, find or make an audio recording of 2 Samuel 11:1–12:7. You may use a Bible-on-tape series or have someone who is not involved with your class record a reading of the passage. (This will allow the youth to hear the Scripture in a voice less familiar to them, which may help them to listen more closely to the story.) Before listening to the reading, give paper and pencils to the youth and ask them to listen carefully to the reading and make a list of things that they think the characters did that were wrong. Ask them to consider the following questions:

- What mistakes did the characters make?
- What actions or choices might they want to revisit?
- Who was harmed?

Play the recording and encourage youth to write as they listen. When the story ends, allow a few minutes for youth to continue writing if necessary.

OPTION B

Needed: Bibles, blankets or towels

Distribute Bibles to all of the youth and help them find 2 Samuel 11:1–12:7. Ask one participant to represent David, and have him or her sit on the floor. Divide this long story into its major scenes and invite four other youth each to read David's part in one of the scenes.

- Scene One—David and Bathsheba (2 Samuel 11:1–5)
- Scene Two—David and Uriah (2 Samuel 11:6–13)
- Scene Three—David and Joab (2 Samuel 11:14–27)
- Scene Four—David and Nathan (2 Samuel 12:1–7a)

As the story is read, ask the youth to listen for times when David makes a mistake and tries to cover it up. When they hear a cover-up, have them go to the person playing David and cover his or her head with a blanket or towel, and to keep adding blankets or towels as the story progresses. At the end of the story, when Nathan says, "You are the man," remove the blankets covering David. Ask the person playing David to talk about how it felt to be under the blankets and how it felt to have the blankets removed.

Reacting to the Story
(5–10 minutes)

OPTION A

If you chose Option A under "Setting the Stage" above, you may want to use the following exercise for this segment.

Needed: newsprint and markers or chalkboard and chalk

Play the reverse form of "The $10,000 Pyramid" again. (This game is described in "Setting the Stage," Option A.) This time, the category is "Mistakes David Made." Draw a six-block pyramid on the newsprint or chalkboard again and invite youth to name the mistakes David made that are mentioned in this story. Try to come up with at least six. If you name more, list these as well. Then ask the youth to decide which mistakes were the most serious and which were the least serious. Redraw the pyramid, placing the least serious mistakes on the bottom and the most serious one on the top. Try to reach a consensus about this matter, but if you cannot, invite youth to rank these mistakes as they believe they should be ranked and to draw their own versions of the pyramid.

OPTION B

Needed: "David Hurt Everybody" handouts

Explain to the youth that in this story, four major characters come into contact with King David: Bathsheba, Uriah, Joab, and Nathan. Point to the four corners of your meeting space and invite youth who wish to focus on Bathsheba to go to one corner, Uriah to another corner, Joab to another corner, and Nathan to the last corner. Give a copy of the "David Hurt Everybody" to each of the youth. Invite them to use the handout to help them think about how David's actions hurt the individual whose corner they are in. If your group is smaller than eight, you might ask small groups to focus on two characters or you may decide to work as one large group. When participants have had a chance to determine how David hurt each of these people, invite them to share their findings with the large group. Then ask all of the youth to answer this question: How did David hurt himself?

Connecting to the Story (5–10 minutes)
OPTION A
If you chose Option A under "Reacting to the Story" above, you may want to use the following exercise for this segment.
Needed: pyramid of "Mistakes David Made" from the previous activity
Refer to the pyramid of "Mistakes David Made" from the previous activity. In this activity, youth will be asked to develop a list of alternatives—things David could have done that would have changed the outcome of the situation. If you have a large group, form three or six small groups and assign one or two mistakes to each youth. If you have a small group, work together to name some alternatives. Write these beside each mistake on the pyramid. When you complete this discussion, create another blank pyramid. Label this one "Why David Made Bad Choices." Work together to come up with at least six reasons that David chose bad

alternatives rather than good ones. Write these in the blanks on the pyramid.

OPTION B
Invite the youth to play "You Are the Counselor." Form pairs and ask one youth in each pair to be David and one to be a counselor. The counselor should ask questions that allow the David to explain his actions, motivations, regrets, and so on. After a few moments, have the pair switch roles. This time the person who was the counselor will play the role of the David and vice versa. Allow a few minutes for the pairs to talk. Then talk together about this experience, using some of the following questions:
■ What happened when you tried to talk about this?
■ Was it easier to play the part of David or the part of the counselor?
■ How was Nathan like a counselor for David?
■ How was Nathan not like a counselor for David?

Exploring the Story (10–15 minutes)
OPTION A
Needed: Bible study resources, such as commentaries on 2 Samuel, Bible handbook, Bible dictionary
Invite the youth to try to get a sense of the cultural constraints on the lives of the people in the passage. The purpose of this activity is not to try to justify or rationalize what characters in this passage did; the purpose is to help us better understand the issues they were facing. Use a Bible commentary, a Bible handbook, or a text that describes life in biblical times. Look for

information about everyday life in David's day. Background can help clarify the actions of the characters from their own perspective. Possible questions you may explore include: What is the role of women? What is the relationship of the prophet to the king? What kind of authority does a king have? What happens to those who defy him?

There are also several idiomatic expressions that mean more than they say. You may wish to try to discover the significance of the following expressions: "In the spring of the year, the time when kings go out to battle" (2 Samuel 11:1); "wash your feet" (2 Samuel 11:8).

OPTION B
Needed: Bibles, "The Life and Times of David the King" handouts
Distribute copies of "The Life and Times of David the King" handout. Read the list of major events in David's life and ask if youth are familiar with them. If you come across stories that the youth have not heard, invite them to read the stories in Scripture, or invite someone who does know the story to summarize it. Beside each situation, indicate whether it was a positive experience (plus sign) a negative experience (minus sign) or a neutral experience (circle).

**Living the Story
(5 minutes)**
OPTION A
Needed: Bibles or photocopies of Psalm 51
Close by asking youth to recall all the mistakes David made during this period of his life. Ask them to think about how David would have

felt: How might he have responded to God at this time? Would he be embarrassed or ashamed? Would he try to hide from God?

Psalm 51 is traditionally seen as David's response to his affair with Bathsheba, the murder of Uriah, and the death of the first son that Bathsheba bore. It is the basis for many songs. To close the session, invite the youth to sing a song based on these verses, or simply read the psalm aloud. Make the psalm a prayer of confession for the participants. Invite them to pray silently or aloud, asking forgiveness for things they regret, things that cannot be undone by human hands.

OPTION B
If you chose Option B under "Exploring the Story" above, you may want to use the following exercise for this segment.
Invite youth to think about the ups and downs of the previous week. Ask them to close their eyes. Have them give a thumbs up, thumbs down, or fist for each day, depending on whether it was a positive day, a negative day, or a neutral day. Assure them that you will be the only person who sees how they respond. Call out each day of the previous week, beginning with Monday. Keep track of the number of positive, negative, and neutral days represented in the group. When you finish going through the week in this manner, ask the youth to open their eyes and give them the totals. Then ask the youth to tell you what the life and times of King David say to them in the ups and downs of their lives.

Close with prayer, thanking God for what you have learned today and for God's presence in all the times of our lives.

Things to Ponder

This is a fascinating story fit for network soap operas. It makes great drama, and youth are not likely to be bored by it. Try not to be too concerned if youth want to delve into the sordid details. This is part of the story, and understanding the seriousness of what David did will help them understand the story more completely. There may be questions about whether Bathsheba agreed to commit adultery or was forced to do so because David was king. Because Bathsheba never speaks, we do not know what she was feeling when she was approached by King David. We do know, however, that she wept bitterly for her husband. This is the only window into her soul that we are given, and it is a picture of a person who is distraught with grief.

Looking Ahead

The next session focuses on a parable unique to the gospel of Luke: the story of the rich man and Lazarus. The rich man appeared to be enjoying the blessings of God while Lazarus seemed cursed with misfortune. The rich man later seemed surprised that he should have been concerned for the poor beggar at his gate. Is there an expectation, or even a responsibility, for people with abundant resources to care about people in need?

David Hurt Everybody

One mistake led to another. One cover-up led to another. Pretty soon, David's actions were out of control. How did David hurt these people?

Bathsheba

Uriah

Joab

Nathan

How did David hurt God?

The Life and Times of David the King

Some of the big events in David's life are listed below. Mark a plus sign by each positive experience, a minus sign by each negative experience, and a circle by each neutral experience.

_____ David is anointed by Samuel: 1 Samuel 16:1–13.

_____ David fights Goliath: 1 Samuel 17:1–54.

_____ David becomes Saul's armor bearer: 1 Samuel 18:1–9.

_____ David becomes a mercenary soldier: 1 Samuel 23:1–14.

_____ David spares Saul's life: 1 Samuel 24:1–22.

_____ David becomes king of all Israel: 2 Samuel 5:1–16.

_____ David brings the ark into Jerusalem: 2 Samuel 6:1–23.

_____ First son of David and Bathsheba dies: 2 Samuel 12:16–23.

_____ Absalom, David's son, revolts and is killed: 2 Samuel 16:1–23.

_____ David places Solomon on the throne: 1 Kings 2:1–9.

7. They Won't Listen

Bible Story: Luke 16:19–31

A Story behind the Story

You may be familiar with Aesop's fables. They are a collection of stories, featuring human characters and talking animals, that teach wise lessons about human behavior. Aesop was a legendary figure, perhaps a slave who won his freedom and entertained Greek nobility in the court of King Croesus (sixth century B.C.). His fables were renowned for their "morals," a concise phrase at the end of the story that summed up the main point and underscored the lesson to be learned.

The Scripture passage in this session is what Jesus called a "parable." Parables were stories that Jesus created to teach his disciples and others certain spiritual truths. They are about the kingdom of God (Matthew 13:24–30), preparedness (Matthew 25:1–13), mercy (Luke 10:30–37), prayer (Luke 11:5–8), God's love (Luke 15:11–24), and many other topics. The parable was filled with persons, objects, and details that were familiar to the hearers. Jesus talked about farmers, landowners, slaves, kings, wedding parties, sheep, families, and so on. His hearers would recognize the setting of the story and the actions of the characters and be drawn in to listen further. Though a few parables clearly rely on the hearer's (and now the reader's) interpreting many of the details (for example, the parable of the landowner and the unfaithful servants, Mark 12:1–9) most have a central point to make. It is important not to be distracted by details that seem strange (such as a farmer who sows seeds without first plowing the ground, Mark 4:3–8), or behavior that seems odd (such as a shepherd who endangers the whole flock for the sake of one sheep, Luke 15:4). We have to keep our focus on why Jesus is telling the story and on the point he is trying to get across. The parable is meant to be a simple story with an easy, obvious solution. When people hear the story and believe they know the answer to its concluding question, they are eager to speak up. Then Jesus is able to challenge them: "If you know the answer, then you should behave that way. You should put it into practice." Parables gave Jesus an opportunity to engage people who came to him with an insincere agenda (such as the lawyer who asked, "Who is my neighbor?" Luke 10:25–29). Once they were engaged, he could direct them to matters of consequence.

Enter the Story

The parable of the rich man and Lazarus is a reversal-of-fortune story. People of faith in Jesus' day believed that God blessed the righteous and cursed the wicked. A corollary of that saying might be, "If a person looks blessed they must be righteous, and if they look cursed they must be wicked." At first sight, the rich man in the parable would appear to be blessed with wealth (covered in purple, verse 19) and Lazarus cursed with misfortune (covered with sores, verse 20). However, after death, their

POSSIBLE YOUTH CONTACT POINTS

- Am I like the rich man or like Lazarus?
- How do I respond to people in need?
- Do I even notice the needs of others?
- What is important to me?

YOU MAY NEED

- two colors of 3" x 5" cards
- special treats
- "Aesop's Fables" handouts
- Bibles
- photocopies of Luke 16:19–31 or several copies of the same translation of the Bible
- newsprint and markers or chalkboard and chalk
- simple art supplies (paper, markers, colored pencils, paint, and so on)
- news magazines, newspapers, or pictures of wealthy and poor people from the Internet
- poster board
- glue
- Bible study aids, such as a concordance and Bible dictionary
- "Opposites" handouts

situations are reversed. This parable challenges the hearers to question their assumptions about appearance and action (or failure to act) and the consequences of misjudging. As you read this story, consider your own place within it and invite God to challenge you. What is God's message for you in this story?

Setting the Stage (5–10 minutes)
OPTION A
Needed: two colors of 3" x 5" cards, special treats
Take two colors of 3" x 5" cards or cut cards from two different colors of construction paper. You may use any two colors; these instructions will use red and blue. As learners enter the room, give each person a card, but stack the deck so that there are twice as many blue cards as red. Announce that those holding red cards will receive special privileges today. Prepare two seating areas—one with many comfortable chairs (red) and a second with insufficient, uncomfortable chairs for those holding the blue cards. Give members of the red group special treats and do not give any to the blue group. Compliment the red group and ignore the blue group. Do several other things for the privileged (red) group and be nonresponsive to the other (blue) group.

OPTION B
Needed: "Aesop's Fables" handouts
When most of the youth have arrived, asked them if they have ever heard of Aesop's fables. If so, ask them to recall some of these stories. Then form several small

groups of youth and assign each group one of the fables included in the handout. Allow time for the youth to read the fable assigned to them and talk about what the moral might be. Then ask the groups to tell their fables and what they think the fables mean. Invite other youth to suggest other possible morals for each fable. When you have talked about all of the stories, have a general discussion about the purpose of fables. Ask questions such as:

- Why were fables told?
- Who was supposed to hear them?
- What sort of behavior did they encourage?
- Do you agree with these morals? Why or why not?

Telling the Story (5 minutes)
OPTION A
If you chose Option A in "Setting the Stage" above, you may want to use the following exercise for this segment.
Needed: Bibles
Assign the two colors to the two characters in the parable: the rich man (red) and Lazarus (blue). Read Luke 16:19–31 aloud, one verse at a time. As you read, invite each group to act out the verses that apply to them without using any words. The red group should act out the parts dealing with the rich man and the blue group should act out the parts dealing with Lazarus. As you prepare for this activity, continue to emphasize the special privileges of the red group ("You, my wonderful and talented friends, are going to play the part of a rich

50

man). Continue to pay less attention to the other group ("Play this part"). There are many surprises in this story and youth may be caught off guard by what happens to the characters. As they act out the story, try to notice how groups are responding to it. When you finish reading the story, switch the seating arrangements and put the blue cardholders into the privileged section and give them whatever the red cardholders received previously (treats or compliments, and so on). Send the red group to the less privileged section of the room. Then talk together about why it is appropriate for the two groups to switch places.

OPTION B
Needed: Bibles (all in the same translation), or photocopies of Luke 16:19–31
Give Bibles to the youth and help them find Luke 16:19–31. Invite the group to participate in an inverted reading. In this form of scripture reading, one person reads all of the spoken parts and everyone else reads the narration together. Choose one person (it may be the leader) to read the parts of the rich man, Lazarus, and Father Abraham, and have the rest of the learners read the narration aloud.

Reacting to the Story (5–10 minutes)
OPTION A
Needed: newsprint and markers or chalkboard and chalk
Tell the learners that Luke 16:19–31 is a parable. Explain that a parable is a simple story with a deep and significant message. Jesus often told

parables when he wanted to illustrate a complex truth or make an important point. Ask the learners to summarize what they think the point of this parable is and to express those thoughts in short statements like the morals of Aesop's fables (examples in "Aesops' Fables" handout). Encourage the youth to come up with many possibilities. Do not be satisfied with a single answer. Make a list of all the statements on the newsprint or chalkboard.

OPTION B
Needed: simple art supplies such as paper, markers, paint, colored pencils, and so on
Begin by asking the youth to answer this question: What was the most surprising thing in this story? Invite a few of them to share their responses. Then distribute paper and art supplies and invite the youth to draw or depict something in this story that seems surprising to them. Allow a few minutes for youth to complete their art work. Then invite them to share what they have drawn and why that surprised them in this story. Be open to a variety of responses and remember to thank each person for his or her contribution.

Connecting to the Story (10–15 minutes)
OPTION A
Needed: news magazines, newspapers, or pictures of wealthy people and poor people printed from the Internet; poster board, glue
Prior to the session, gather newspapers or magazines that feature

pictures of extremely wealthy and extremely impoverished people. You may find similar pictures on the Web. Lay these before the youth and invite them to cut out pictures of people who remind them of the rich man or Lazarus. Glue these pictures to the poster board to form a group collage. When the collage is complete, read the story again, pointing to pictures of wealthy people when you read about the rich man and to pictures of poor people when you read about Lazarus. After reading, ask the youth to talk about seeing these faces. How do they feel about the story now? What is the moral of this story for our world?

OPTION B
If you chose Option A under "Setting the Stage" above, you may want to use the following exercise for this segment.
If you formed privileged and underprivileged groups at the beginning of the session, ask the youth to return to those groups now. Have the less privileged (blue) group sit in the privileged section. Have the privileged (red) group sit in the less privileged section. Ask the less privileged group (blue) to try to read this story as a story for the rich man and to consider its message for people like the rich man. Ask the privileged group (red) to read this story as a story for Lazarus and to consider its message for people like Lazarus. Allow a few minutes for the two groups to work on this project separately. Then discuss together the following questions:

- Was it hard to look at the story this way?
- What is the message for the rich man?
- What is the message for Lazarus?
- What is the message for us?

Exploring the Story (10–15 minutes)
OPTION A
Needed: newsprint and markers or chalkboard and chalk
This story is a study in contrasts. Draw a line down the middle of a piece of newsprint or a chalkboard. Invite the youth to read the story again and call out all of the contrasts present in the story. Here are a few examples:
- Rich man's expensive clothes/ Poor man's sores
- Rich man's fine food/ Poor man's crumbs
- Rich man in hell/ Poor man with Abraham

Read through the entire passage looking for these contrasts. Then invite one youth to be the rich man and one youth to be Lazarus. Ask Lazarus to talk about what he needed from the rich man. How could the rich man have helped him? Then ask the rich man to talk about what he needed from Lazarus. How could Lazarus have helped him?

OPTION B
Needed: Bible study aids, such as a concordance and Bible dictionary
Tell the group that Jesus often talked about wealth and money. Take some time to discover how many times Jesus referred to these important topics and what Jesus

had to say about them. Give the participants a concordance or Bible dictionary and ask them to look up topics such as the following: wealth, wealthy, money, poor, riches, treasure. Talk together about what you discovered. Then discuss the following questions:

■ Why did Jesus talk about money?

■ What main point did he want to get across?

■ What is more important than money, according to Jesus?

Living the Story (5–10 minutes)

Read the "Looking Ahead" section. If you want to do this project for the next session, set aside 5–6 minutes in this section to discuss what the group will do.

OPTION A

If you chose Option A in "Setting the Stage" or "Telling the Story" above, you may want to use the following exercise for this segment. Have a period of prayer that focuses the needs of the two groups symbolized by the two colors. Begin with a sentence and invite others to speak from the two perspectives. For example: Hold up a red card (the rich man) and offer a prayer sentence such as, "Sometimes we are the privileged. Help us, Lord, to see beyond our front gate and not ignore those in need." Invite others to share sentence prayers. Then hold up a blue card (Lazarus) and offer a prayer sentence such as, "Sometimes we are the poor and weak. Strengthen us, Lord, and remind us of your love." Invite others to share prayer sentences.

OPTION B

Needed: "Opposites" handouts, markers

Give each youth a copy of the "Opposites" handout and a marker. Allow time for them to draw an outline of their hands and write some of their personal characteristics on the fingers. Then invite them to tape the handouts to a window so that the back side faces them. Ask them to use a marker to draw a reverse image of their hands, following the outline they made earlier. Remove the handout from the window and write characteristics that are not like them in the fingers of the reverse image. Ask youth to reflect on ways for them to connect with people who are not like them. What role can these people play in their lives? How might they need these people, just as the rich man needed Lazarus?

Ask the youth to take the handouts with them as a reminder to look for ways to be in relationship with people who are not like them. Close with a time of prayer.

Things to Ponder

Your group may be filled with people like the rich man or it may be filled with people like Lazarus. More likely, you have some of both as part of your group. Be sensitive to these realities during this session. If you choose to form privileged and less privileged groups ("Setting the Stage" Option A), be sure to include both wealthy and poor youth in each group. If the subject of monetary wealth comes up, remind the youth that everyone living in the United States lives in wealth when compared with people in many parts of the world. This is a story for everyone, not just for a select few.

Looking Ahead

The next lesson deals with a practice of the early church to supply the needs of the less fortunate in their community. There may be members of your church or community who are sick, shut-in, lonely, or in need. Think about something the youth could put together for such a member and ask them to bring a contribution for this project to your next session. For example, they may bring pieces of fruit or flowers that can be combined or arranged into gifts that the class can carry to the member; they may bring toiletry items for persons in a shelter; they may bring simple toys for children in a hospital. Consider the option that will require the participants to do more than just bring money. They should do something that helps them connect to the person the gift is for.

Aesop's Fables

The Bundle of Sticks

Once there was a wise farmer whose quarrelsome sons drove him almost to distraction. One day he called them to his room. Before him lay a bundle of sticks tied together. Each one of his sons in turn was commanded to take the bundle and break it in two. They all tried but failed. Then the father untied the bundle and gave them each a stick to break, one by one. This they did with the greatest ease. "My sons," he said, "as long as you remain united you are a match for your enemies, but when you quarrel and become separated, you can be destroyed."
Moral: In unity there is strength.

The Fox and the Grapes

Mister Fox was just about famished, and thirsty too. He came to a vineyard where the sun-ripened grapes were hanging up on a trellis in a tempting show, but too high for him to reach. He took a run and a jump, snapping at the nearest bunch, but missed. Again and again he jumped, only to miss the luscious prize. At last, worn out by his efforts, he retreated, muttering, "Well, I never really wanted those grapes anyway. I am sure they are sour and perhaps wormy in the bargain."
Moral: Any fool can despise what he cannot get.

The Boy and the Filberts

A boy put his hand in a pitcher, which contained a goodly quantity of figs and filberts. Greedily he clutched as many as his fist could possibly hold. But when he tried to pull it out, the narrowness of the neck of the vessel prevented him. Unwilling to lose any of the nuts, yet unable to draw out his hand, the lad burst into tears, bitterly bewailing his hard fortune. An honest fellow standing nearby gave him this wise and reasonable advice: "Grasp only half the quantity, my boy, and you'll succeed."
Moral: Half a loaf is better than no bread.

The Fisherman Piping

There was once a fisherman who enjoyed playing on the bagpipes as much as he did fishing. He sat on the riverbank and played a tune hoping that the fish would be attracted and jump ashore. When nothing happened, he took a casting net, threw it into the water, and soon drew it forth filled with fish. Then as the fish danced and flopped about on shore, the fisherman shook his head and said, "Since you would not dance when I piped, I will have none of your dancing now."
Moral: To do the right thing at the right season is a great art.

Source: *Aesop's Fables* (New York: Grosset and Dunlap Publishers, 1963).

Opposites

The rich man and Lazarus had almost nothing in common, and yet each could have helped the other in significant ways. In the space below, draw an outline of your hand and write something about yourself on each finger. On the reverse side, draw a reverse image of your hand and write opposite traits on each finger.

8. Why Has Satan Filled Your Heart?

Bible Story: Acts 5:1–11

A Story behind the Story

The Acts of the Apostles, the fifth book of the New Testament, follows the four Gospels in theme as well as in fact. It sketches the growth and development of the church from a small group of 120 Jewish men and women on the day of Pentecost (Acts 1:13–15; 2:1–4) to a large international community reaching all the way to Rome (Acts 28:16–31). Those early believers witnessed the power of the Holy Spirit. They experienced the fulfillment of Old Testament prophesies (Acts 2:16–21), and they saw miracles of healing (Acts 3:1–8; 9:32–34; 14:8–11), boldness in testifying (Acts 3:12–26; 4:8–12) and deliverance from the hand of their adversaries (Acts 4:16–21; 12:5–11). They knew the heights of the glory of God. Yet, though they had been lifted by these glimpses of the heavenly, they did not lose touch with their earthly brothers and sisters. In their ecstasy, they did not forget the depths of human need. They were sensitive and responsive to widows and orphans, the poor and outcast, all those whom Jesus called "the least" (Matthew 25:42–45). They saw the wonders of God firsthand, and that experience culminated not in attitudes of selfishness or superiority but in love and concern for one another.

Several passages describe the characteristics of these early believers. "They devoted themselves to the apostles' teaching and fellowship, to the breaking of bread and the prayers" (Acts 2:42). The Acts of the Apostles depicts a community that was aware of the predicaments of its members (4:32–35). Those who had property or possessions sold them and made their resources available to the apostles. Peter and the rest of the Twelve accepted the responsibility of serving the poor and needy until the church's increased numbers and diversity called for other arrangements (Acts 6:1–7). In Acts 4:36–37, the generosity of Barnabas is singled out as an example of a common practice. The members of this early Christian community put their faith into action by sharing possessions with those who were in need. The story of Ananias and Sapphira is presented as a contrast to the generosity of the other believers.[1]

Enter the Story

As you prepare the participants to hear this story, consider two items. First, although the central characters are far from role models, we shouldn't lose sight of what they were asked to do. Christians are called to show compassion for others because God has already shown compassion for us. Be prepared to encourage the youth to do service as a response to God's grace and mercy. If they volunteer out of guilt or an attempt to gain recognition, they will miss the true rewards that come not only from helping others but from opening the heart and learning to care about others.

Second, reflect on what this story says about crime and punishment. Ananias and Sapphira received a quick judgment on their misdeeds.

57

POSSIBLE YOUTH CONTACT POINTS

- **Where do I look for opportunities to serve others?**
- **In what ways can I serve others?**
- **What is the proper use of my possessions?**
- **Do I demonstrate compassion for those who have less?**
- **What do I do to impress others?**
- **Am I honest with God and with others?**

YOU MAY NEED

- **gifts to share with someone else (see "Looking Ahead" from the previous session)**
- **Bibles**
- **identical copies of Acts 5:1–11 for group reading**
- **props, costumes, video camera for silent film (optional)**
- **TV/VCR**
- **pencils or pens**
- **newsprint and markers**
- **chalkboard and chalk**
- **parallel Bible (an edition containing more than one translation) or several Bibles, a variety of translations**
- **Bible concordance with dictionary**
- **hymnals or songbooks**
- **wrapping paper, ribbons and bows**
- **scissors**
- **"Inventory Sheet" handouts**
- **"Parallel Reading" handouts**

There are always consequences for our actions, but the proximity of deed and reward are not always so close or so clear. It is easier to have an ethical discussion about this infamous couple because they were caught. Be prepared to discuss issues of fairness around such questions as, "Why do some people get away with doing wrong and others are punished?" "Why should I try to do right when everyone does wrong and no one seems to care?"

Setting the Stage (5–10 minutes)
OPTION A
Needed: gifts brought by the youth
At the close of the previous session, youth were asked to bring gifts that could be shared with people in need. It may be wise to call the youth during the week to remind them of what they were supposed to bring. Before the youth arrive, set up an area where the gifts they are bringing may be displayed. As youth arrive, invite them to display what they brought. When everyone is present, invite the youth to talk about what they brought and why. If some youth forgot to bring gifts, talk together about other items that might be needed or other ways to participate in this service project. Comment on how each gift makes the whole a greater presentation than one gift alone. Remind the youth that they are acting as a community. When all the gifts are assembled, invite the learners to sit and prepare to hear the Scripture.

OPTION B
Talk with youth as they arrive about what is going on in their lives. When most youth have arrived, invite them to play "What do we have in common?" Arrange chairs in a circle and invite the youth to be seated. Explain that the purpose of this game is to make as many people as possible stand up by naming something they have in common. Tell them they may name places they've been, experiences they've shared, aspects of their common identity or heritage, objects of clothing, or whatever they believe will make the most people stand. Start the game yourself or ask one of the youth to begin by standing and naming something the group members may have in common. Ask those sharing what was named to stand. Then ask everyone to be seated, and ask the person to the left to stand and name something. Continue around the circle until everyone has had a turn. When you complete the game, talk together about some of the things you have in common. Ask the youth which items surprised them. Ask questions such as:

- What other things do you have in common?
- Do you prefer to be with people with whom you have much in common, or do you prefer the company of people who are different than you?

Telling the Story (5–15 minutes)
OPTION A
Needed: Bibles, props and video camera for silent film (optional)
Before reading the story, ask the youth to talk about some of the characteristics of silent films (no dialogue, exaggerated body language,

theater organ playing melodramatic background music, signs that explain what is happening, and so on). Invite the group to prepare a silent film of the story from Acts 5:1–11. Assign the youth to play the parts of Peter, Ananias, and Sapphira. If you have a large group, you might invite some youth to develop background music for the film and others to develop signs that will describe the action. If you wish, you may prepare these signs ahead of time to speed the process along. The remaining participants will play the members of the church. Allow a few minutes for the youth to read the passage and develop their parts. Ask the participants to use exaggerated motions and facial expressions as they react to what happens in the story. Encourage them to get into their parts and enjoy what they are doing. Be sure that the players look at one another as they act out their parts. Try to take note of the verses that cause the most interesting reactions. If you have access to a video recorder, tape the action and prepare to play it for the next segment.

OPTION B
Needed: identical photocopies of Acts 5:1–11
Give youth copies of Acts 5:1–11. Explain that you will be doing a "crescendo reading." This is a method for group reading of Scripture in which readers are added gradually so that the volume of the reading gets louder and louder. Organize the group before you begin the reading. Assign one person to read verse one and add readers gradually verse by verse. If you

have a small group, you may ask them to begin with low voices and allow their voices to get louder as the reading progresses. Be sure that everyone is reading by verse 11. When you have organized the reading, present it. Then, if time permits try a "decrescendo reading." Begin with the entire group reading the story and end with only one person. Talk together about which reading seemed most appropriate to the story and why.

Reacting to the Story (5 minutes)
OPTION A
If you chose Option A under "Telling the Story" above, you may want to use the following exercise for this segment.
Needed: video of the silent film made by the youth (optional), TV/VCR
If you were able to record the "silent film" the youth made as you were telling the story, play it now for the youth and talk together about the presentation. If you did not videotape your performance, work together to try to recall it. Talk together about some of the following questions:
■ Which verses caused the most interesting facial expressions?
■ Which verses were hardest to portray? Why?
■ Did you like this story?
■ Would it make a good movie? Why or why not?

OPTION B
Needed: three chairs labeled "yes," "no," and "maybe"
Use three chairs to create a straight line—one chair at either end of the

room and one in the middle, creating a continuum with one end being "yes," the other end, "no," and the middle, "maybe." Make small signs to mark these positions. Read the following statements or other statements that you would like to present and ask the learners to move silently to the appropriate part of the room to reflect their answers. After everyone has made a decision, ask a few learners to share briefly why they are standing where they are. Then present the next statement. Possible statements include the following:

- Ananias and Sapphira were bad people.
- Peter came down on them too hard.
- Ananias and Sapphira were greedy.
- Ananias and Sapphira were trying to impress people.
- Ananias and Sapphira hurt the church by their actions.
- The punishment Ananias and Sapphira received was appropriate.
- If this happened to someone I knew, I would be afraid.

Connecting to the Story (10 minutes)
OPTION A
Needed: "Inventory Sheet" handouts, pencils
Ananias and Sapphira were asked to bring an offering to the church so that the church could carry out a ministry to those in need. Explain to the group that an inventory is a list of items that a store or business has on hand ready to use. Invite them to think about their own personal inventory. What do they have on hand, ready for God to use?

Give the youth each a copy of the "Inventory Sheet" handout and invite them to take stock of themselves. In one column, they should make a list of what they have. In another column they should describe how they use what they have—at church, at school, at home, in the community, at work, or wherever this ability or gift is used. In the third column, they should list other ways they could use what they have—things they could do with these gifts that they are not already doing. Allow a few minutes for youth to work individually on this handout. Then invite each one to choose a partner and share his or her chart. Ask them to consider the following questions:

- What am I dedicating to God?
- What am I holding back?
- What talents have I shared in other places but not at church?
- What gifts do I offer at church but not at school?"

OPTION B
Needed: paper and pencils
Form small groups of two to four youth and invite them to rewrite this story as if it were happening today. The names and individuals involved in their retelling should be fictional—no real people! Ask the writers to consider how people might hide what they have to give, what would happen if people hiding money were confronted by the pastor, what would happen to the pastor, and how other people in the church or community might respond. Allow a few minutes for the groups to prepare an alternate version. Then invite groups to share what they created.

Exploring the Story
(10–15 minutes)

OPTION A

*Needed: Bibles, two large
sheets of paper, markers*
The story of Ananias and Sapphira
follows a description of the early
church's generosity in Acts 4:32–37.
These verses record the believers'
owning possessions together and
sharing generously with anyone
in need. Invite one of the youth
to read Acts 4:32–37 aloud. Then
write "Ananias and Sapphira"
on one large sheet of paper and
"Believers" on the other. Post the
sheets of paper where everyone can
see them. Invite the participants
to call out descriptive words or
phrases that describe either Ananias
and Sapphira or the other believers.
Write these on the appropriate
pieces of paper. After a few minutes,
or when you have several descriptions for each, talk about what you
see. Ask questions such as:

■ How do these two groups of
people differ?

■ What motivates each to do what
they do?

■ Which group are we most like?

■ Does a believer ever turn into
someone like Ananias and Sapphira? How?

OPTION B

*Needed: various translations of
the Bible, "Parallel Reading" handouts, commentaries on Acts, Bible
dictionary or concordance*
Read the story of Ananias and
Sapphira from various translations
of the Bible, including versions
representing the traditional (the
King James Version, the Revised
Standard Version, or the New

International Version) and the more
dynamic translations (the Living
Bible, Today's English Version, or
the Contemporary English Version).
Read the passage one verse at a
time from each translation. As you
read, you may notice that some of
the words are translated differently.
Make a list of these words as you
read. When you complete the reading, give each youth a copy of the
"Parallel Reading" handout. The
handout lists words that are translated differently in various versions
of the Bible. It also lists the word
in its Greek form, the language in
which the New Testament was written, and a rough translation of that
Greek word. Invite the youth to
look together at some of the words
listed on the handout and discuss
how they might translate them into
their own language, using words
that they use regularly and that
would make sense to their friends.
Do the same with other words you
discovered from your reading. Look
them up in a Bible dictionary or
concordance that offers a definition
of the Greek word. When you complete this activity, ask the learners
to talk about the process of trans-
lating. Ask: How would you translate this story for a contemporary
audience?

Living the Story
(5–10 minutes)

OPTION A

*If you chose Option A under "Con-
necting to the Story," you may want
to use the following exercise for this
segment. If you did not choose that
option, give a copy of the "Inventory Sheet" handout to each youth
and invite them to use it as a guide*

for considering what they might offer to God in the coming week.
Needed: information from "Inventory Sheet" handouts
Invite the youth to use information from their handouts to choose a gift, talent, or activity that they want to rededicate to God. It may be in an area in which they are already involved at church. It may be something they normally do at home or school that they had not connected to their faith and now want to offer to God. Ask a few, who are comfortable doing so, to speak their pledges out loud. Close the session with prayer, asking God to empower all to keep the promises made, spoken or unspoken.

OPTION B
If you chose Option A under "Setting the Stage" above, you may want to use the following exercise for this segment.
Needed: items youth brought to share with someone
Refer to "Looking Ahead" from the previous session. The purpose of this project is to do an act of kindness and remembrance for someone. Take time to involve everyone in a discussion on how to proceed with performing this service. You may want to talk about the tasks to be done and ask for volunteers to do the specific work. For example, the gifts have to be assembled, wrapped or decorated, and transported. The date and time of visitation should be determined. Also plan a time, after the project is completed, for evaluating what was learned. To close the session, sing a song that addresses the unity of believers in Christ, such as, "We Are One in the

Spirit," "We're Marching to Zion," or "One Voice." After singing, gather in a circle and invite each youth to share one thing he or she will remember from the session.

Things to Ponder
The early church saw to the need of its own members and of the poor of the community. Just as Ananias and Sapphira were bad examples of a demonstration of caring, so Barnabas was a positive example (Acts 4:36–37). Acts of kindness often go unnoticed and unrewarded by the world at large. Consider how tempting it is to do something for attention, admiration, or even fame. Jesus was tempted by the devil to draw attention to himself for the wrong reasons, and he resisted doing so (Matthew 4:5–7). As we show compassion, we may also be tempted to "show off for the camera."

Looking Ahead
The next session explores the call of Jesus to "fish for people." Several of the options work with this fishing theme. Try to gather nets and other fishing gear to create a nautical atmosphere in the room. Fish crackers and tuna are recommended, and several of the options suggest the use of Go Fish cards. You can do all of the options without making these preparations, but gathering these items during the week and using them will help the youth get into the story.

Note
1. William Barclay, *The Acts of the Apostles,* The Daily Study Bible Series, Revised Edition (Louisville, Ky.: Westminster Press, 1976), 43.

Inventory Sheet

It's time to take stock. What do you have on hand in your personal inventory that you might be able to share with others? Use the categories below to prompt your thoughts. Try to list something in each category.

	What I Have	**How I Use It**	**How I Could Use It**
Activities (things you do)			
Abilities (things you do well)			
Personality (something special about you)			
Possessions (things you own)			
Time (where you spend your time)			

What could God do with this inventory?

Parallel Reading

ACTS 5:1

King James Version—possession
New International Version—property
New Revised Standard Version—property
New Century Version—land
Contemporary English Version—property
Word in Greek—*ktema*
Definition—an acquisition, something that one has acquired
My language—

ACTS 5:5

King James Version—gave up the ghost
New International Version—died
New Revised Standard Version—died
New Century Version—died
Contemporary English Version—dropped dead
Greek—*ekupscho*
Definition—to expire
My language—

ACTS 5:9

King James Version—tempt
New International Version—test
New Revised Standard Version—test
New Century Version—test
Contemporary English Version—test
Greek—*periazo*
Definition—to test
My language—

OTHER WORDS:

9. You Will Be Catching People

Bible Story: Luke 5:1–11

A Story behind the Story

Luke 5:1–11 presents the calling of the first disciples—James and John, who are the sons of Zebedee, and Simon. This story is repeated in the other gospels, but Luke's account is very different. First, Luke does not mention Andrew, the brother of Simon, whereas Matthew and Mark both do. In Matthew and Mark, Jesus saw Simon and Andrew and invited them to follow him. Luke adds more detail. In Luke's account, Jesus climbed into Simon's boat and taught the multitudes of people who had gathered on the shore. After teaching the crowds, Jesus asked Simon to go out to the deeper waters to try to catch fish. Simon explained that he had fished all night but caught nothing. Still, Simon agreed to do what Jesus asked, in spite of his own reluctance. He was rewarded for his obedience to Jesus with a magnificent catch.

Simon's declaration to Jesus, "yet if you say so" (Luke 5:5), and his subsequent compliance to what Jesus asked seem to indicate that Peter already knew Jesus and had established a trusting relationship with him. In the preceding chapter (Luke 4:38–39), Jesus was present in Simon's home and healed his mother-in-law. She immediately arose and served those around her. Matthew and Mark also give the account of the healing of Simon Peter's mother-in-law, but place it after Peter has been called as a disciple. In Luke's gospel, this encounter with Jesus led to a trusting relationship that perhaps helped Simon respond to Jesus with obedience.

Simon was so astonished by the huge amount of fish he caught that he fell at Jesus' knees and confessed his sinfulness. The miracle caused the disciples to examine their own lives and wonder about their worthiness to be in the presence of this holy man. Jesus told them not to be afraid. Then he said an interesting thing: "From now on you will be catching people" (Luke 5:10). When they heard this, Simon, James, and John all left everything and followed him.

"Catching people" has become a metaphor for bringing people into relationship with Jesus Christ. This story provides a model for how that process takes place. The experiences of these first disciples parallel the experiences of Jesus' current disciples—trusting in Jesus, obeying his commands, confessing sin, and following him. Just as Jesus called the first disciples, he also calls each of us.

Enter the Story

Begin your preparation for this session by praying. Thank God for the words that you will read and ask for understanding and guidance. Feel God's presence as you listen for direction and read the story.

Read Luke 5:1–11 silently and then read it aloud. Reflect upon the story. Is the story familiar to you?

Section Three

Salvation
by Dotty Abney

- In what ways am I obedient to God?
- When am I reluctant to obey?
- What does "catching people" mean?
- Do I know people who need to be "caught"? Who are they?
- What does it mean to follow Jesus?
- Do I follow Jesus?
- Do others follow me?
- Whom do I trust? Why?

YOU MAY NEED

- bowl of Goldfish crackers
- one or two cans of tuna, can opener
- fishing nets or items from boats
- pencils
- blank sheets of paper or large index cards
- Bibles
- deck of "Go Fish" cards or regular playing cards for every three to four youth
- "Fishing for People Word Search" handouts
- newsprint and marker
- paper plates and crayons
- "Whom Do You Obey?" handouts
- topical Bible, commentaries on the Gospels, Bible dictionary
- ball of yarn
- candle
- matches
- coffee can partially filled with sand
- glass of water

Who are the characters? Think about what they may have looked like. As commercial fishermen, were they dark from toiling in the sun? Were their hands callused from pulling in the rough nets? What is the setting? Was the lake of Gennesaret a freshwater lake or saltwater lake? What kind of fish might they have caught? What might the boat that Simon Peter used have looked like? How do you relate to this story? Have you had a similar experience of calling? What has Jesus asked you to do?

Think of the youth who will be attending this session. Imagine them hearing this story for the first time. How might they interpret the story? Be open to whatever catches the attention of the youth.

Setting the Stage (5–10 minutes)

Needed: bowl of Goldfish crackers, one or two cans of tuna, can opener, fishing nets or other items from boats (optional)
Before youth arrive, open cans of tuna, discard the lids, and place them somewhere in the room where they will not be easily observed. If you have access to pieces of equipment from boats, arrange them around the room.

Greet youth as they enter the room. Be certain that introductions are made for any newcomers. Invite the youth to sit in a circle and share the Goldfish crackers. As the bowl is being passed, ask youth what they notice in the room that is unusual. See if they mention the nets or the fishy odor of tuna. They may offer their own interpretations of the significance of the props.

OPTION A

As you prepare the youth to hear today's story of the fishermen Simon, James, and John, invite the youth to tell some "fish stories." Have several volunteers from the group tell two true facts and one untrue (fish story) about themselves. Allow the group to guess which statements are true and which ones are not. After a few youth have shared, ask the group to consider that listening is an important part of interpreting. Recalling prior knowledge can be helpful in the interpretation process as well. Point out to the youth that these techniques can also be important in interpreting today's Bible story.

OPTION B

Needed: pencils, blank sheets of paper or large index cards
As you prepare the youth to hear a story about three people who left everything and followed Jesus, give each youth a pencil and a sheet of paper or a large index card. Instruct them to write down their answers to the questions that you will ask. First, ask the youth what it means to follow someone. Allow them time to consider their response. Next, ask the youth who they follow in their own lives. Give them a moment or two to write their answers. Some examples for youth might be: parents, friends, teachers, their minister, and so on. Ask the youth to write down characteristics or traits of the people that they have listed. When the youth have completed their responses, ask for volunteers to share the information they have written. Point out to the

youth that these questions may be helpful in interpreting today's Bible story.

Telling the Story
(5–10 minutes)
OPTION A
Needed: Bibles, a deck of "Go Fish" cards or regular playing cards for every three to four youth
Distribute Bibles to the youth and help them find Luke 5:1–11. Before reading the story, tell the youth that it is very important for them to listen carefully to the story and try to remember what happens. Ask for a volunteer to read the story while others read silently in their Bibles. At the end of the story, put the Bibles away.

Form groups of three or four youth. Remove the ones (or aces), twos, and threes from the deck. (You may use these in "Reacting to the Story," Option A.) Invite each youth to draw a card from the deck, being careful to note the number that is on the card. Instruct the youth to retell today's Bible story in their group by taking turns adding a sentence. Each youth's sentence should be composed of the same number of words as the number on the card he or she just drew. Encourage youth to enjoy this activity as they use their own words to remember the story.

OPTION B
Needed: pencils, "Fishing for People Word Search" handouts
Give each youth a pencil and a copy of the handout entitled, "Fishing for People Word Search." Explain to the youth that this word search has words from today's Bible story

hidden in it. Words are horizontal, vertical, and diagonal. Tell the youth that you will be reading the Bible story of Luke 5:1–11 to them. Encourage them to listen very carefully to the story. As they recognize one of the words from the story and see it on the word search, they are to circle the letters of that word. (The words hidden in the puzzle are: lake, Gennesaret, boats, nets, Jesus, Simon, people, fish, followed, James, John, and Zebedee. Most translations include all of these words, but be sure to check your version of Scripture before you read it.)

Begin reading the story. Read slowly so that the youth are able to hear and understand the words. As one of the words from the word search is introduced, you might want to hesitate so that the youth will have sufficient time to circle the letters on their puzzles. Allow youth to work together if necessary. When you have finished reading the story, invite the youth to share their answers with the group.

Reacting to the Story
(5–10 minutes)
OPTION A
If you chose Option A under "Telling the Story," you may want to use the following exercise for this segment.
Needed: the ones (or aces), twos, and threes from a deck of "Go Fish" or regular playing cards
Ask the youth to sit in a large circle. Hold the ones (or aces), twos, and threes face down in front of the youth and invite each youth to draw a card. Explain to the group that you are going to ask questions

about the story and that you will ask youth who are holding a particular number to answer them. Say something such as, "If you are holding a two, tell us your answer to this question." Be sensitive to the fact that some youth may not feel comfortable answering some questions. If necessary, rephrase a question or ask another question so that all youth can participate. Suggested questions include:

- Who is your favorite character in this story and why?
- What surprised you the most about the story?
- Which person or group of people in the story are you most like?
- Why do you think Simon was willing to do what Jesus asked?
- What else would you like to know?

OPTION B
Needed: newsprint, marker, paper plates, crayons
Display newsprint in a location that can be seen easily. Begin by asking the youth to call out emotions that you can list on the newsprint. Answers might include happiness, sadness, doubt, surprise, anger, confusion, and embarrassment. After several of these are listed, instruct the youth to use the crayons to draw simple faces on the paper plates. Suggest that they draw one emotion on one side of a plate, and another on the opposite side. Encourage the youth to draw as many of the emotions listed on the newsprint as possible.

Read the Bible story again, inviting youth to hold up a plate that represents their reaction to a particular part of the story. For instance, some youth might be surprised at the number of fish that were caught, and some might be confused as to why the fishermen followed Jesus. Assure the youth that there may be conflicting emotions and several plates may go up at the same time.

Connecting to the Story (5–10 minutes)
OPTION A
Needed: a deck of "Go Fish" or regular playing cards for each group of three to four youth
Form groups of three to four youth. Place a deck of cards face down in the center of each group. Do not deal the cards at this time. Tell the groups that you are going to read a series of statements that relate to the story. If the statement is true for them, they should take one card. If it is not true for them, they should take two cards. Read statements such as:

- I know who Jesus is.
- I believe in Jesus.
- I listen to what Jesus says.
- I try to do what Jesus asks me to do.
- Sometimes, it is hard to do what Jesus asks me to do.
- I have seen Jesus do amazing things in my life.
- I know some people who do not know Jesus.
- I am seeking to follow Jesus.

After reading the statements, if time permits, invite the groups to play "Go Fish" with the cards they drew. After playing the game, talk together about the statements.

OPTION B
Needed: pencils, "Whom Do You Obey?" handouts
Give each youth a copy of the handout "Whom Do You Obey?" and a pencil. The left portion of the handout asks the question, "Whom do you obey?" and the right portion of the handout asks, "Why are you obedient?"

Ask the youth to begin listing the persons that they obey. Examples might be parents, teachers, older siblings, police officers, government officials, and so on. Encourage the youth to consider their lists carefully. Allow time for them to complete the lists.

Now ask the youth to complete the right portion of the handout, writing the reasons for their obedience to each person they have listed. Examples for this portion might include love, respect, admiration, trust, fear, or habit. Again, allow the youth time to reflect upon their answers and write their responses.

When they have finished the top portion, direct their attention to the last question on the handout, "Why was Peter obedient to Jesus?" Give the youth time to complete this final question, which invites their opinion or interpretation. Ask the youth to compare their own reasons for obedience to Peter's possible reasons for obedience. Encourage the youth to share their answers with the group.

Exploring the Story
(10–15 minutes)
OPTION A
Needed: pencils and paper or index cards, Bibles, topical Bible,

commentaries on the Gospels, Bible dictionary
Ask the youth to work with a partner for this exercise. Encourage them to explore today's Bible story in greater detail. Point out the various resources that you have gathered to aid in deeper exploration of the story. Briefly describe how each resource might be used (e.g., a topical Bible could be used to discover other passages related to specific themes in the story; commentaries explain how others have interpreted the story or a particular portion of it; and a Bible dictionary defines specific concepts or elements in the story in relation to their ancient context).

Ask the youth to discover if this story of the calling of the first disciples is located in the other three Gospels. Invite them to compare the stories and take notes about what they find. They might wish to look at what precedes the story in each Gospel and compare that as well. Ask them to look in the commentaries and discover why stories might differ.

As the youth finish their explorations, you may want to gather in a group and have them share their discoveries.

OPTION B
Needed: Bibles, pencils, paper, and Bible study aids such as commentaries and Bible dictionaries
Invite the youth to explore the characters in this story more deeply. Form two groups, one to examine the life of Simon and the other to examine the lives of James and John.

Point out to the youth that in today's Bible story, all three fishermen "left everything and followed him" (Luke 5:11). Invite the group looking at Simon to read Luke 4:38–44. In this passage, Jesus heals Simon's mother-in-law. Ask the group to write a script depicting what might have happened when Simon explained to his family that he was leaving everything and following Jesus. Ask the group looking at James and John to reread Luke 5:10–11 and then to write a script in which James and John tell their father that they are leaving everything and following Jesus.

Encourage both groups to use biblical commentaries or dictionaries to help in their research. Ask both groups to assign parts and plan to act out their scripts. When the groups have finished, invite them to present what they have written to the total group.

**Living the Story
(5 minutes)**
OPTION A
Needed: ball of yarn
Ask the youth to stand in a circle and join you in weaving a net. Hold the ball of yarn in your right hand. Unwind some of the yarn and hold the end tightly in your left hand. Explain to the youth that you will be tossing the ball across the circle to one of them. Each person who catches the yarn will need to share one thing that they learned about following Jesus from today's story. The youth will then hold the yarn tightly and throw the ball to another person.

Begin the process by sharing what you learned about following Jesus from this story. Then hold tightly to the end of yarn as you toss the ball, making the first line of the net across the circle. When one of the youth catches the ball of yarn, ask him or her to share what he or she learned about following Jesus from today's story. That youth should then unwind a portion of the yarn, hold the string of yarn securely in the left hand, and toss the ball across the circle to another youth. The process is repeated to weave the net. Encourage youth to toss the yarn to every person in the circle.

When you have completed the exercise and everyone has had an opportunity to participate, invite the youth to join you in lifting your hands, thus lifting the net. Close in prayer thanking God for allowing us to follow Jesus.

OPTION B
Needed: small pieces of blank paper, pencils, candle, matches, coffee can partially filled with sand, glass of water
Light the candle and place it next to the coffee can. (As a precaution, you may want to stand by the candle with a glass of water at hand.) Give each participant paper and a pencil. Point out to the youth that as we follow Jesus, we may want to leave some things behind, such as fears, doubts, problems, or conflicts. Invite the youth to think about their own lives and write down what they would like to leave. Point out to the youth that no one will see what they have written.

As they finish writing, encourage the youth to come forward, catch their papers on fire, and then drop them into the can. Close in prayer thanking God for sending Jesus to us.

Things to Ponder

This story invites youth to consider their faithfulness as followers of Jesus and whether they are "catching people" as Jesus taught his followers to do. At some point in the session, try to define what "catching people" means. Discuss ways that they might invite their friends to meet Jesus, ways that your church seeks to tell others about Jesus, or personal experiences you have had as you have tried to share your faith with others.

Looking Ahead

The next session is the story of Jesus walking on the water and Peter's attempt to walk on the water also. A storm frightens the disciples while they are in a boat on the Sea of Galilee. "Telling the Story," Option A, leads youth through the use of guided imagery. If you plan to use this option you will need a CD or cassette recording of sounds of the ocean or a thunderstorm.

Fishing for People Word Search

```
A  G  E  N  N  E  S  A  R  E  T
B  L  I  O  E  E  I  N  E  T  S
O  Z  A  M  M  M  M  F  P  W  F
A  X  A  A  L  O  O  I  J  B  O
T  J  J  F  E  N  N  S  O  R  L
S  I  C  H  A  O  P  H  H  Y  L
U  L  A  K  E  X  W  C  N  V  O
Z  E  B  E  D  E  E  S  Y  A  W
Q  T  H  L  N  P  E  O  P  L  E
V  C  G  J  E  S  U  S  N  K  D
```

"Whom Do You Obey?"

Whom do you obey?	Why are you obedient?
1.	1.
2.	2.
3.	3.
4.	4.
5.	5.
6.	6.

Why was Peter obedient to Jesus?

10. Lord, Save Me

Bible Story: Matthew 14:22–33

A Story behind the Story

In Matthew 14:22–33, Jesus walks on the water and Peter attempts to do so. Right before this event, Jesus fed the five thousand with five loaves and two fish. Jesus dismissed the crowd and sent the disciples by boat on ahead to the other side. He then "went up the mountain by himself to pray" (Matthew 14:23). The winds increased and the disciples' boat was battered by the waves. By early in the morning they were far from land, but Jesus approached them—walking on the water! Matthew implies that even though Jesus was not with the disciples, he knew of their fear and need for him, and he went to them. At a time in their lives when many youth do not know whom to trust, this story is a shining example of the trustworthiness of Jesus.

Matthew also relates that when Peter faltered and began to sink in the water, he cried out to Jesus. "Jesus immediately reached out his hand and caught him" (Matthew 14:31). This is another example of Jesus' trustworthiness. Even though Peter took his eyes off Jesus, noticed the strong wind, and faltered, Jesus reached out to him immediately.

A third demonstration of Jesus' great love and concern for the disciples may be seen in Matthew 14:32. When Jesus and Peter got into the boat, the winds ceased. Once again it appears that Jesus was meeting the needs of the disciples. The disciples worshiped him, saying, "Truly you are the Son of God" (Matthew 14:33).

In this passage, Matthew does not directly identify the body of water that the disciples are crossing. The verse that immediately follows the story does identify the setting however. "When they had crossed over, they came to land at Gennesaret" (Matthew 14:34). The city of Gennesaret is located on the Lake of Gennesaret, often called the Sea of Galilee. Matthew refers to the Sea of Galilee when he tells the story of the calling of the first disciples in chapter 4, verse 18. Luke refers to the Lake of Gennesaret when he tells of the calling of the first disciples in chapter 5, verse 1. Refer to a New Testament map or map of Palestine to see the location of the Lake of Gennesaret.

Enter the Story

Begin your preparation for this session by praying. Thank God for the opportunity of leading youth as they discover God's Word. Ask God to give you understanding and direction as you read the words of the story.

As you prepare for this session, find a place and time where you can be alone to read Matthew 14:22–33 and reflect upon it. If you have a recording of sounds from the ocean or perhaps the sounds of a thunderstorm, you might want to play it while you read. Have a pencil and paper with you so that you can make notes about the story.

Is this story familiar to you? What about this story is appealing or interesting? Are there characters in the story with whom you identify? Think of the emotions involved in this story that might be similar to emotions you have experienced. Enormous fear, tremendous trust, and Peter's risk taking are all parts of the story.

Consider the youth who will be attending this session. With which characters might they identify? Which emotions might they have experienced? Pray for the youth as they interpret this story.

Setting the Stage (5–10 minutes)

Welcome the youth as they come into the room. Invite them to sit down and visit with one another. You might ask them about their week at school or perhaps about their family or friends. Do they have concerns they would like to share with the group?

OPTION A
Needed: blindfolds
As you prepare the youth to hear today's story of Peter's trust in Jesus, invite them to participate in a "trust walk." Have each youth pair up with a partner. Explain that one of the partners will be blindfolded. The other partner will take the blindfolded one for a brief walk, perhaps around the room or down the hall. Point out to the youth that they should take great care of their blindfolded partners, making certain to keep them safe. Some youth will feel more comfortable holding the hand of their partner. Suggest that those acting as guides should encourage their blindfolded partners to touch objects in the room and try

to identify them, and to listen for other people's voices and try to identify them. Explain to the participants that they will have only a few moments for this exercise in trust, and then they will be reversing roles. Those who were blindfolded will then become the guides.

When the youth finish this activity, ask them how it felt to be dependent upon someone else. Trusting can be a difficult experience for some. Allow the youth to discuss their feelings.

OPTION B
Needed: pencils, blank sheets of paper or large index cards
As you prepare the youth to hear today's story of Peter's brave attempt to walk on water, give each youth a pencil and a sheet of paper or a large index card. Explain to the youth that you would like them to consider the question "What is the bravest thing you have ever done?" for a few moments in silence. Then ask them to write about the experience. Give them several moments to complete this task. When everyone has finished, ask for volunteers to share their story with the others. You might ask youth to reflect upon their experience in a new way. Was trusting a part of their experience?

Telling the Story (5–10 minutes)

OPTION A
Needed: cassette or CD of sounds of the ocean or a thunderstorm, cassette or CD player, electric fan
Explain to the youth that you will be reading the Bible story of Matthew 14:22–33 and that you

POSSIBLE YOUTH CONTACT POINTS
- What does trustworthy mean?
- Am I trustworthy?
- How deep is my faith?
- How do I falter in my faith?
- Am I a risk taker?
- Can I trust Jesus to be with me?
- What makes it difficult for me to trust Jesus or to trust others?

YOU MAY NEED
- blindfolds
- pencils
- blank sheets of paper or index cards
- cassette or CD of sounds of the ocean or a thunderstorm
- cassette or CD player
- electric fan
- video camera (optional)
- "How Deep?" handouts
- "Can You Find It?" handouts
- Bibles
- colored pencils or markers
- New Testament maps, topical Bible, commentaries on the Gospels, Bible dictionary
- small container such as a bowl or vase
- large candle
- a small candle for every youth
- matches

75

will lead them to experience the story through guided imagery. Start the recording of sounds from the ocean or a thunderstorm. Position the electric fan and turn it on so that the youth can feel its breeze. Ask the youth to close their eyes as you read the story. Encourage them to listen to the words and to imagine the crashing of the waves, the sting of the wind on their faces, the loud boom of thunder, the rocking of the boat, and so on. Invite them to visualize the setting of the story, seeing the colors and textures of the scenery. Invite them to visualize the characters, how each might have looked and reacted to the events in the story.

Read the story slowly so that the youth might hear and experience the words. Allow time for the youth to create their own mental picture of each scene; allow the story to come alive for the youth.

OPTION B
Needed: pencils, paper
Suggest that the youth gather around a table and be seated for this activity in order for them to be able to write more easily. Give a pencil and a sheet of paper to each youth. Explain that you will be reading Matthew 14:22–33. Invite the youth to become newspaper reporters for the reading of this story. Ask them to take notes as they hear the words. Point out that a good reporter always gets the "who," "what," "when," "where," and "why" of the story. Remind the youth that they will need to listen carefully to get all of the information.

Read the story slowly, pausing between verses so that the youth

can recognize and understand the information. Be sure all the participants have enough time to write down what they are hearing.

When you have finished reading the story, wait for the youth to finish writing. Then ask them if they need you to repeat any of the story for them. Allow time for them to complete their notes.

Reacting to the Story (5–15 minutes)
OPTION A
If you chose Option A under "Telling the Story" above, you may want to use the following exercise for this segment.
Begin by asking the youth if they were able to create mental pictures for themselves as they listened to the story. Ask questions such as: Could you feel the wind? Did you experience the rocking of the boat? Did you hear the crashing of the waves? Then encourage youth to share their images of the story. Ask questions such as: Did you see Jesus walking on the water and believe that he was a ghost? Did you feel terror at this prospect? Were you relieved that Jesus found you and came to you as you were tossed about in the storm? Was Peter so trusting of Jesus that he actually thought he could walk on the water also? Why did Peter start to sink? Did he struggle as he was sinking? Encourage youth to share what they saw themselves as they were listening to the story. Ask about the emotions they experienced. Their interpretation and images may differ greatly from yours and from the others in the class. Be open to their reactions to this story. Some youth

will be very comfortable in sharing their experience, while others may not be. Allow each youth the opportunity to speak.

OPTION B

Needed: video camera (optional)

If you chose Option B under "Telling the Story" above, you may want to choose the following exercise for this segment.

Begin by telling the youth that they will continue in their roles as newspaper reporters. Ask them if they were able to discover the "who," "what," "when," "where," and "why" of the story. Invite them to pretend that they are part of a local news team and are to give an eyewitness report. Encourage them to read through their notes and prepare a brief account. Allow a few moments for the youth to organize their notes and plan what they will say.

Ask for volunteers to share their reports. You might want to record their statements with a video camera. If so, enlist a youth to be the camera operator and another youth to be the director by calling out, "Action" and "Cut" when the reporter has completed the account. Some youth will really enjoy this chance to act. Others may be more reluctant. Encourage all the youth to participate in whatever way they feel most comfortable.

Connecting to the Story (5–15 minutes)

OPTION A

Needed: pencils, "How Deep?" handouts

Give each youth a pencil and a copy of the "How Deep?" handout. Explain that the handout is designed to measure how much they have immersed themselves in Christian faith. Point out that attending church could be considered one of the beginning stages of faith. It is symbolized by being ankle-deep in water. Participating in Christian organizations outside of church is symbolized by waist-deep water. Telling of your faith to others is symbolized by even deeper water. Ask the youth to consider their own faith journeys.

Next, ask the youth to list the risks involved in these levels. Some examples might be: being called names, being laughed at, not being invited or included in certain activities, and so on. Some youth may have experienced some of these reactions. Invite them to share their thoughts with the group.

Ask the youth to look at the handout and fill in the gauge identifying their present faith status. Invite the youth to share their answers, and encourage them to continue in their faith journeys.

OPTION B

Needed: pencils, paper

Give each youth a pencil and a sheet of paper. Ask them to recall ways that Jesus demonstrated trustworthiness in today's story. Encourage them to voice their interpretations aloud.

Explain to the youth that they will be making a time line of their own lives. Instruct them to draw a horizontal line with hash marks, and beside these hash marks to write their age at different times in their lives. They might begin with an age that they can remember, possibly three or four years old. Explain to the youth that they will be identifying people that they trusted during those times. For example, at three years of age they probably trusted their parents. At seven years of age they may have trusted their Sunday school teacher or minister. At fifteen, they may have trusted their best friend or team coach. Allow the youth time to complete this task.

When they have finished, encourage them to share their responses with the group. Ask: What makes a person trustworthy?

**Exploring the Story
(10–15 minutes)**
OPTION A
Needed: pencils, "Can You Find It?" handout, Bibles
Invite the youth to explore today's Bible story in greater detail. Give each youth a pencil and a copy of the "Can You Find It?" handout. Explain that they can find the answers to each of the questions on the handout by reading today's Bible story, found in Matthew 14:22–33. Point out to the youth that they may also need to read the passage that precedes today's story.

Allow several moments for the youth to complete the handout. As they finish their explorations, you may want to gather in a group and ask the youth to share their discoveries. Discuss ways that the story of the feeding of the five thousand relates to this story.

OPTION B
Needed: New Testament maps, colored pencils or markers, paper, Bibles, topical Bible, commentaries on the Gospels, Bible dictionary
Suggest that the youth gather around a table and be seated for this activity

in order for them to be able to draw and write more easily. Invite them to enjoy exploring today's Bible story in greater detail. Point out the various resources that you have gathered to aid in deeper exploration. Briefly describe how each resource might be used (e.g., a topical Bible to discover other passages related to specific themes in the story, commentaries to find out how others have interpreted the story or a particular portion of it, a Bible dictionary to explore specific concepts or elements in the story in relation to their ancient context, New Testament maps to discover the cities surrounding the body of water in today's story.)

Invite the youth to draw a map of the setting from today's Bible story. Instruct them to read the passage of Scripture that immediately follows the story of Matthew 14:22–33 for a clue as to the city located on the body of water where today's story took place. They may need to use commentaries or the topical Bible to discover that the body of water is Lake Gennesaret, which is sometimes called the Sea of Galilee. Provide paper and colored pencils so that each youth can draw the Sea of Galilee and the surrounding areas. When the youth have finished, encourage them to share their maps with the group. Talk together about what they learned through this activity.

**Living the Story
(5 minutes)**
OPTION A
Needed: pencils, small pieces of blank paper or index cards, a small container such as a bowl or vase
Distribute a pencil and a small piece of blank paper or index card to

each youth. Invite the participants to write down a time in their lives when they were frightened and could feel the calming presence of Jesus. Explain to the youth that they will not be showing what they have written to anyone. When they have finished writing, instruct them to fold the paper and place it in the bowl or vase. Allow a couple of minutes for the youth to do this.

When all the youth have finished, invite them to stand in a circle with you and hold hands. Ask them to join in silent prayer, thanking Jesus for his presence. Maintain silence for a few moments, and then close with "Amen."

OPTION B
Needed: large candle, one small candle for each person including yourself, matches
Light the large candle and explain to the youth that this candle symbolizes the presence of Jesus Christ. Point out that we do not worship the candle itself, but use it to remind ourselves of Christ's presence with us.

Encourage each of the youth to find a partner. If there is an odd number of youth, pair yourself with one of them. Instruct them to spend a few minutes visiting with their partners and asking them about special prayer concerns or special joys they would like to share. Some partners may choose to go into a corner of the room, giving themselves a little distance from others while they are sharing special concerns. Allow approximately two minutes for their conversations with one another. Then quietly call the youth back to the group circle. Ask them all to say a silent prayer for the concerns they have heard from their partners. Tell them that as they each finish praying, they may light one of the smaller candles using the flame from the Christ candle and then leave in silence.

Things to Ponder
There are many opportunities for the youth to share their personal experiences in today's session. Be sensitive to the fact that the youth will bring different types of experiences to the conversation. Some may have been in church all of their lives, while others may attend infrequently or may have only recently begun attending.

Looking Ahead
The next session is the story of Peter's denial of Jesus. It is a dramatic story and may have great impact on the youth who are hearing it. "Telling the Story," Option B, calls for a guest speaker to read the passage of Matthew 26:31–35,69–75. If you plan to use this option, you will need to recruit a speaker. You might want to invite someone with a dramatic flair or experience in public speaking.

Can You Find It?

What well-known Bible story comes before this story in Matthew 14:22–33?

How large was the crowd of people that Jesus dismissed in the beginning of the Scripture?

After Jesus sent the disciples on ahead to the other side, what did he do?

At what time of day did Jesus approach the disciples?

Why were the disciples initially frightened of Jesus?

What was Jesus' response to the disciples when they were afraid?

When Peter faltered and began to sink, what did Jesus do?

As Jesus calmed the wind and the disciples were no longer afraid, what words of praise did they use as they worshiped Jesus?

How Deep?

Think of the Christian life as this swimming pool. Where are you swimming? How deep is the water? Where do you want to swim? What are the risks involved in each level?

I go to church—sometimes.

I attend church activities, and I'm getting to know Jesus.

I'm trying to help others know Jesus.

11. I Do Not Know the Man

Bible Story: Matthew 26:31–35,69–75

A Story behind the Story

Peter's denial takes place in the context of the Passion of Jesus, which includes the time of the Last Supper (Matthew 26:17–30); Jesus' prayer in Gethsemane (Matthew 26:36–46); his appearance before the high priest, the Jewish authority (Matthew 26:57–68); his trial before Pilate, the Roman authority (Matthew 27:1–2,11–23); and his agonizing death on the cross (Matthew 27:24–56). In the midst of the tremendous Passion of Jesus, we find the minor passions of Judas and Peter—a time of tremendous emotional, spiritual, and physical stress. Peter's passion is his denial of Jesus, while Judas's is his betrayal of Jesus. One cannot help but compare Peter's denial (Matthew 26:69–75) with Judas' betrayal (Matthew 26:47–56).

What is the difference between betrayal and denial? Judas's betrayal ultimately leads to the death of Jesus and also Judas (Matthew 27:3–10). Peter's denial ultimately leads to bitter tears (Matthew 26:75). Judas's betrayal is a premeditated act for some sort of gain (Matthew 26:14–16), while Peter's denial is a spontaneous response to the sheer terror of being identified with someone who is about to be condemned to death. Although Matthew reports that Judas repented of his actions (Matthew 27:3–10), he did so too late to save Jesus from condemnation or death.

Peter's denial, on the other hand, did not affect Jesus' condemnation or death. It affected Peter's image of himself as a faithful follower of Jesus, especially in the light of his bold promise to be true and loyal: "Even though I must die with you" (Matthew 26:35). When faced with the possibility of harm, Peter denied even knowing Jesus.

Youth may easily relate to this sort of denial. When afraid of exclusion from the crowd, a young person may be tempted to deny that Jesus is important or real or worthy of absolute allegiance. When faced with a choice between the Way of Jesus and the way of popular culture, youth may be tempted to deny Jesus in order to escape ridicule or even condemnation by those following the popular way. In moments of stress and fear, youth may say with Peter, "I do not know the man."

Enter the Story

Begin your preparation for this session by praying. Ask God to guide you as you read the story and search for understanding. Pray for insight and direction, and prepare to feel God's presence as you read.

Read Matthew 26:31–35,69–75 silently and then read it aloud. Consider the emotions that Peter must have felt. Did he seem confident of his allegiance to Jesus in the beginning of the story? Was he later paralyzed with fear that led him to deny knowing Jesus? Was he overcome with grief and self-loathing at the end of the story? Are these emotions that youth may have experienced?

Think of the youth who will be attending this session. Imagine them hearing this story for the first time. How might they react and interpret this story? This is a dramatic passage and one that can be sobering for us to hear. Pray for the youth who will be attending this session.

Setting the Stage
(5–10 minutes)

Greet youth as they come into the room. Allow them the opportunity to greet each other as well. Invite the youth to sit down and be comfortable. Lead the youth in an opening prayer, asking God to be present and to provide guidance and understanding.

OPTION A

Needed: pencils, blank sheets of paper or large index cards

As you prepare the youth to hear today's Bible story of Peter's denial of Jesus, give each youth a pencil and a blank sheet of paper or a large index card. Ask the youth to reflect on the following questions:

■ Have you ever disappointed a friend or a family member?

■ Can you recall a time when you let a friend or family member down?

■ How did this happen?

■ What were the consequences?

Encourage the youth to think about their experience for a few moments and then write about them on the paper that you have provided. Allow time for the youth to record their responses.

When all the youth have finished writing, ask for volunteers to share what they have written. Some youth will be willing to share their experience, while others may not. Give each volunteer the opportunity to speak.

OPTION B

As you prepare the youth to hear today's Bible story, give them the opportunity to share with one another one of their experiences from the previous week. Ask them to share something they did that made them either feel good about themselves or feel bad about themselves. Allow a few moments for the youth to think about their week. Begin by sharing an experience from your own week. Then ask for volunteers or begin with the youth seated on your right and go in a circle, allowing each youth the opportunity to speak. You may want to ask questions or invite the youth to clarify details. Remember, however, that these are their stories and their opportunity to relate them. Some youth will find this an easy task and be willing to share their experience. Others may feel less comfortable and be reluctant to speak. Be sensitive to the needs of the youth as you encourage them to participate.

Telling the Story
(5 minutes)

OPTION A

Needed: chalice or Communion cup

You might like to have the youth gather around a table and be seated for this activity. Tell the youth that you will be reading Matthew 26:31–35, 69–75 and that this Bible story is a series of conversations. Explain that you are using a chalice or Communion cup for this activity because the Last Supper immediately

POSSIBLE YOUTH CONTACT POINTS

■ **What is denial?**

■ **In what ways do I deny that I know Jesus?**

■ **What are the consequences of denying Jesus?**

■ **What is the Passion of Jesus?**

■ **Where do I experience peer pressure?**

■ **Am I afraid of peer pressure?**

■ **Does Jesus forgive me?**

YOU MAY NEED

■ pencils

■ blank sheets of paper or index cards

■ chalice or Communion cup

■ guest speaker (see "Telling the Story," Option B)

■ "Speakers" handouts

■ magazines

■ glue

■ construction paper

■ scissors

■ "Many Hurts" handouts

■ Bibles, topical Bible, commentaries on the Gospels, Bible dictionary

■ small brown paper sacks

■ trash can

■ small scraps of brown felt or construction paper

■ white paper with the outline of a cross drawn on it

precedes this story. Instruct the youth that each time the speaker changes, the person holding the chalice or cup should pass it to the person seated on his or her right. Explain that it might be a speaker that they have heard earlier in the story. They should pass the chalice or cup each time the speaker changes, not only when a new speaker is introduced. Encourage the youth to listen carefully in order to hear who is speaking. Give the chalice or cup to one of the youth and begin reading the story. You may want to read slowly and hesitate slightly as the speaker changes.

The speakers are as follows: Jesus (v. 31); Peter (v. 33); Jesus (v. 34); Peter (v. 35); disciples (v. 35b); servant girl (v. 69); Peter (v. 70); another servant girl (v. 71); Peter (v. 72); bystanders (v. 73); Peter (v. 74); and Jesus (v. 75).

When you have finished the story, thank the youth for participating.

OPTION B
Needed: guest speaker
Prior to the session, invite someone from the congregation to tell this story to the youth. The storyteller may use different voices, costumes, or positions to indicate different speakers in the story. Introduce the guest speaker to the youth. Explain to the youth that the speaker will be presenting today's Bible story and reading Matthew 26:31–35,69–75. Encourage the youth to give their attention to the speaker and to listen carefully to the story. Encourage the speaker to make himself or herself comfortable for the presentation and to direct the youth as to where they should sit.

Reacting to the Story (5–10 minutes)
OPTION A
If you chose Option A under "Telling the Story" above, you may want to use the following exercise for this segment.
Needed: pencils, "Speakers" handouts, Bibles
Give each youth a pencil and a copy of the "Speakers" handout. Invite the youth to look at the handout with you. Explain that each of the speakers from today's Bible story is listed on the handout. Peter is listed twice, once for the beginning verses and once for the ending verses. Instruct the youth that they are to draw a line connecting each speaker with the emotions that they believe the speaker may have felt. Point out that they might decide to connect more than one emotion with each speaker. Encourage the youth to open their Bibles to Matthew 26:31–35,69–75 to reflect upon the story. Allow several moments for the youth to complete the handout.

When the youth have finished writing, ask for volunteers to share their answers. The youth will probably differ from one another— and from you—about the answers. Remember that there are no right or wrong answers. This is an opportunity for the youth to react to the story.

OPTION B
Needed: magazines, glue, construction paper, scissors
Gather the youth around a table and have them be seated for this activity. Place the magazines, glue, construction paper, and scissors in the center of the table so that all the youth have easy access to the

materials. Invite the youth to make individual collages of the Bible story that they have just heard. Instruct them to cut out words, people, scenery, objects, and so on that symbolize the story and then to glue these cutouts on a piece of construction paper, making them fit in whatever way they choose. Allow several moments for this activity, announcing when there are two to three minutes left for the activity. Some youth may really enjoy this project and be eager to continue. When the youth have finished, encourage them to share their collages with the group, telling what each picture means to them. Allow each youth the opportunity to speak.

Connecting to the Story (10–15 minutes)

OPTION A

Needed: pencils, blank sheets of paper or large index cards
Explain to the youth that many times we can identify with characters in a story or the circumstances of a story. Invite the youth to consider today's Bible passage. Ask questions such as the following:
■ What would this story be like in today's culture?
■ When faced with peer pressure, have we ever been tempted to deny that Jesus is worthy of absolute allegiance?
■ Have we ever claimed ignorance of Jesus and what he demands of us?
■ Can we identify with any of the characters in today's story and the emotions they may have felt?

Invite the youth to write a contemporary story, factual or fictional, based on today's Scripture, that

they may choose to share or not to share with the group. Allow the youth several moments to write their stories.

When the youth have finished writing, ask whether someone would like to share his or her story. Since these stories may be personal and the youth may feel like they are confessing, they may not wish to disclose them. Be sensitive to the needs of the youth, allowing those who wish to speak the opportunity to do so.

OPTION B
Invite the youth to reflect upon today's Bible story. Encourage them to consider Peter's words to Jesus in Matthew 26:35: "Even though I must die with you, I will not deny you." Encourage the youth to consider what Peter was feeling at that moment of his bold declaration. Invite the youth to discuss times when they too have made bold promises. Examples of this might be: a promise to parents that they would never drink, smoke, break curfew, skip school, swear, and so on; a promise to friends that they would always be there for them, never forget them; a promise to God that they would give up something if he would only answer their prayer. Allow each youth the opportunity to speak and offer an illustration of a bold promise.

Encourage the youth to reflect silently on promises they may have made. Ask questions such as:
■ Did you keep those promises? If not, why not?
■ Did you simply forget?
■ Did you give in to peer pressure?
■ Did you feel afraid of ridicule or condemnation?

Allow youth the opportunity to speak if they volunteer.

Exploring the Story (10–15 minutes)
OPTION A
Needed: pencils, paper, Bibles
Gather the youth around a table and have them be seated for this activity. Form groups of two to four and give each group paper, pencils, and Bibles. Explain that they have been looking at a scene from Jesus' Passion and that "passion" means a time of tremendous emotional, spiritual, and physical stress. Tell the youth that the Bible passages that precede and follow today's Scripture are all part of the Passion narrative. Invite the groups to outline the events of Jesus' Passion, beginning with Matthew 26 and ending with Matthew 27:54. If you need to save some time, assign specific parts of these chapters to each group and work together to make one group outline. Allow the youth several moments to do this.

When the outlines are complete, talk together about the events of Jesus' Passion. Then invite the youth to work in their small groups to rate the difficulty of these events for Jesus on a scale of one to five, giving the events that seem easiest to bear a one and those that seem hardest to bear a five. Talk together about how each group rated these events.

OPTION B
Needed: pencils, Bibles, "Many Hurts" handouts, Bible commentaries
Explain to the group that Peter was not the only person who denied or disappointed Jesus. The arrest and crucifixion of Jesus caused great fear and concern among his disciples, and many people fled from his side. Form groups of two to four and distribute Bibles, pencils, and copies of the "Many Hurts" handout. Ask the groups to look up the Scripture passages listed on the handout, decide who in that passage is hurting Jesus, how they are doing so, and why they are doing so.

When the handouts are completed, talk together about the youths' responses. Remember that there are no right or wrong answers to the how and why questions. The passage that may create the most discussion is Matthew 27:45–46, in which Jesus feels that God has forsaken him. Talk about this passage together, discussing questions such as:
■ Is God letting Jesus down?
■ Is Jesus so overwhelmed with the pain of this experience that he does not see the larger picture?
■ Is Jesus quoting Scripture to fulfill a prophecy?

There are many possible interpretations for this passage. If time permits, look up this passage in biblical commentaries to discover other possible understandings.

Living the Story (5 minutes)
OPTION A
Needed: pencils, paper, small paper sacks, trash can
Give each youth a pencil, a sheet of paper, and a paper sack. Ask the youth to try to recall a time in the past when they said or did something that they now regret. Ask

them to consider this for a few moments and then write a sentence asking God to forgive them. Explain that no one will see what they have written.

When everyone has finished writing, encourage each youth to crumple the sheet of paper, place it inside the sack, and then roll the sack into a ball. Place the trash can in the center of the group and allow each youth to toss his or her "ball" into the trash can. After all the youth have had the opportunity to throw away their trash, call out a hearty "Amen" to close the session.

OPTION B

Needed: randomly shaped scraps of brown felt or brown construction paper, large sheet of white paper with the outline of a cross drawn on it, glue

Tape the sheet of paper with the outline of a cross to a wall or chalkboard. Be certain that the youth will be able to reach it easily. Explain to the youth that they will be making a mosaic by gluing the scraps inside the outline.

Invite the youth to stand in a circle near the cross outline. Ask them to think silently about what they learned today about Jesus' Passion. Invite them to share an insight that they gained from today's conversation—a reason for thanking God, a desire to change something in their own lives, or some other learning. After each youth shares, invite him or her to glue a piece of felt or paper inside the cross.

When everyone who wishes to do so has shared, point out to the youth that although they have filled in part of the cross, some spaces are still present. Likewise, today's session may have filled in some of their understanding about Jesus' death on the cross, but there may still be gaps in their understanding or questions that they still have. Encourage them to think about these questions in the coming week or to share them with you, a parent, a youth leader, or a pastor. Close with a silent prayer of thanks and confession.

Things to Ponder

Today's Bible story of Peter's denial of Jesus is powerful and thought provoking. It may lead youth to some deep reflection and evaluation of their own lives. They may feel that they have disappointed a friend or a loved one. They may even feel that they have denied Jesus. Some youth may have shared personal experiences and may now feel vulnerable or possibly even regret doing so. Consider how you might respond to these youth when the session is over. Try to contact those who might need to talk.

Looking Ahead

The next session is the story of the persecution of Peter and the apostles. For Option B under "Connecting to the Story," the youth will be looking for a connection between the persecution of the early Christians and persecution of persons for their beliefs in more modern times. Examples might include Christians in China or Muslims in Kosovo. You may want to gather news magazines or search the Internet for stories about these situations.

~~~~~

Speakers

Many people speak in Matthew 26:31–35,69–75. Match the following speakers with emotions they may have felt. If you do not agree with any of the choices, write in your own ideas.

Jesus

Disgust

Hatred

Terror

Peter (beginning verses)

Glee

Confusion

Surprise

Disciples

Fear

Resolve

Sadness

Servant Girls

Happiness

Confidence

Anger

Bystanders

Boastful

Depressed

Dedicated

Peter (ending verses)

Alone

Compassionate

Disappointed

Annoyed

Many Hurts

Peter was not the only person who denied or disappointed Jesus. Many people deserted him in those final hours. Read each Scripture. Decide who hurt Jesus, how, and why.

Scripture	Who?	How?	Why?
Matthew 26:36–46			
Matthew 26:47–50			
Matthew 26:51–54			
Matthew 26:54–56			
Matthew 27:15–23			
Matthew 27:45–46			

12. We Must Obey God

Bible Story: Acts 5:12–42

A Story behind the Story

A common theme in Scripture is the persecution that God's people often faced because of their faithfulness to God. But persecution is never the end of the story. Biblical writers always emphasize that God acted on behalf of persecuted people and worked to protect them. Daniel was not harmed by the lions, for God sent an angel to shut the lions' mouths (Daniel 6). Shadrach, Meshach, and Abednego were kept from harm when placed in the fiery furnace (Daniel 3). The arrest of Peter and the apostles in Acts 5:12–42 is another story of God's faithfulness in the midst of persecution. The apostles were imprisoned, but an angel of God set them free.

This story has much in common with other persecution stories found in Scripture. For example, the arrest came about because the high priest was "filled with jealousy" (Acts 5:17). Authorities who felt threatened by the power of God and God's followers are present in other Bible passages as well. Consider King Herod, who was frightened when the Magi told him of the birth of the "king of the Jews" and sought to destroy him (Matthew 2), or King Saul, who feared David because "the LORD was with him" (1 Samuel 18:12).

Peter and the apostles were brought before the council, or Sanhedrin. This body was the official Jewish court and was made up of seventy priests, scribes, and elders, presided over by the high priest. Jesus had been led before the council prior to his crucifixion (Matthew 26:59). The jealous council warned Peter and the apostles not to speak of Jesus again, but they answered, "We must obey God rather than any human authority" (Acts 5:29). Upon their release, the apostles rejoiced that they were "considered worthy to suffer dishonor for the sake of the name" (Acts 5:41). The apostles continued to "teach and proclaim Jesus as the Messiah" (Acts 5:42).

This session's story begins with "Now many signs and wonders were done among the people through the apostles" (Acts 5:12). There are many signs and wonders of God's power in this passage as well as in the preceding four chapters of Acts. Like the early apostles, we can enjoy looking for "signs and wonders" of God's power in our lives!

Enter the Story

Begin your preparation for this session by praying. Thank God for the words that you will read and ask for understanding of the story. Feel God's direction as you prepare to lead the youth.

Read Acts 5:12–42. This is a longer passage and more detailed than the stories of previous weeks. It begins with signs and wonders of God's work through the apostles. The apostles are then arrested and jailed by the jealous council. An angel releases them and the apostles resume preaching in the temple. Again the police bring them before the council. Peter and the other apostles declare that they must obey God rather than any human authority. After deliberation, the apostles are flogged and ordered not to speak of Jesus again. The apostles rejoice in their opportunity to witness and continue to teach and proclaim Jesus as Messiah.

There are many facets of this story with many emotions involved. How might the youth interpret this story? Be open to whatever catches their attention.

Setting the Stage (5–10 minutes)

Greet the youth individually as they come into the room. Invite them to sit in a circle and enjoy visiting. Check in with the youth, asking them about their week. Encourage the youth to share with one another.

OPTION A

Needed: individually wrapped candy of assorted colors such as Starburst Fruit Chews or Gummy Savers, color chart of emotions

Pass the bag of candy around the circle and invite the youth to take a piece. Explain that they should hold their candy and not eat it yet! When all of the youth have chosen a piece of candy, ask them to look at the chart with you. If they drew a pink candy, ask them to tell of a time when they felt embarrassed; if they drew green, to tell of a time when they felt jealous; if they drew red, to tell of a time when they felt angry; if they drew yellow, to tell of a time when they felt afraid. (You may need to vary your chart according to the candy that you have chosen.) Other options might be: happy, sad, lonely, and so forth. The Bible story today involves emotions of jealousy, anger, and joy (rejoicing), so you

might like to include those emotions on your chart.

Ask for volunteers to share their stories with the group. Invite the youth to eat their candy when they have finished their stories.

OPTION B

Invite the youth to think about times in their daily lives when they feel stress. They might feel stressed about their classes, assignments, or tests. They may feel stressed about dating or perhaps not dating. They might have a part-time job that they are worried about. They may be struggling with plans for college, perhaps where they will go or what they will major in. They may feel stressed about finances. They might feel stressed about their sports team. They may feel stressed by peer pressure. Encourage the youth to share their thoughts with the group.

Now invite the youth to consider how they deal with these stresses in their lives. Ask questions such as:
■ Do you talk to friends, talk with parents, counselors or teachers at school?
■ Do you exercise, shop, use deep breathing techniques?
■ Do you pray?

Allow time for the youth to share their ideas with the group.

Telling the Story (5–10 minutes)

OPTION A

Needed: butcher block paper, markers or crayons

Invite the youth to gather around a table and be seated for this activity. Roll out a large piece of the butcher block paper so that it extends the length of the table.

POSSIBLE YOUTH CONTACT POINTS
■ **What is a sign of God's power?**
■ **How do I deal with stress?**
■ **Are Christians persecuted for their beliefs?**
■ **Does God take care of me?**
■ **What frightens me?**

YOU MAY NEED
■ **individually wrapped candy of assorted colors**
■ **color chart of emotions**
■ **butcher block paper**
■ **markers or crayons**
■ **pencils**
■ **"Always, Sometimes, Never" handouts**
■ **magazines such as** *Newsweek,* *TIME,* **and** *U.S. News and World Report*
■ **"Signs and Wonders" handouts**
■ **blank sheets of paper or large index cards**
■ **Bibles, topical Bible, commentaries, Bible dictionary**
■ **strips of brightly colored construction paper**
■ **glue**
■ **pieces of ribbon**

You might wish to tape it. Be sure that each youth can reach the paper and will have a place to draw. Lay out plenty of markers or crayons within easy reach of each of the youth. Explain to the youth that you will be reading today's Bible story of Acts 5:12–42. Invite them to listen to the words carefully and as you are reading to draw or doodle on the paper. Point out that they may wish to draw certain characters in the story or perhaps certain words. They may wish to create a scene or several scenes. Explain to the youth that this is a long story and they may draw several pictures. Encourage the youth to continue listening even as they are drawing, so that they will not miss parts of the story.

Read the story slowly so that the youth will have time to draw and capture on paper their initial reactions to the story.

OPTION B
Explain to the youth that you will be reading today's Bible story from Acts 5:12–42. Point out that this story is lengthy and has several scenes. Invite the youth to participate in a type of responsive reading. Ask them to say the words "Praise God" in unison each time they hear a positive statement from the Scripture. As an example, tell them that the first sentence, "Now many signs and wonders were done among the people through the apostles," is a positive statement and they would respond with "Praise God." The account of the apostles' arrest and imprisonment in verses 17 and 18 is not a positive statement; therefore, they would not respond with "Praise God."

Read the story slowly and hesitate after positive statements. Leave the decisions about when to respond up to the youth, however. Some youth may call out "Praise God," while others do not. Some youth may be exuberant in their participation, while others may feel more reluctant. Encourage the youth to enjoy listening to the story and participating.

Reacting to the Story (5 minutes)
OPTION A
If you chose Option A under "Telling the Story," you may want to choose the following exercise for this segment.
Needed: "group doodle" from Option A in "Telling the Story" above
Begin by standing or sitting close to the "group doodle" that the youth have just completed. Invite the youth to share what they have drawn. You might do this by going around in a circle and encouraging each youth to show which drawing or doodle is theirs. Encourage the youth to point at their drawings or to portions of them while they are talking. Allow each youth time to explaining what he or she drew. Ask questions such as:
■ Did the color you chose have any significance to you?
■ Why did you choose this particular character, word, or portion of the story?

You may be surprised by their answers! Be open to their reactions to the story.

Some youth may have drawn several doodles while others may have drawn only one. Allow each youth the opportunity to speak. You may want to display the "group doodle" on the wall when you have finished.

OPTION B

If you chose Option B under "Telling the Story," you may want to choose the following exercise for this segment.
Begin by asking the youth if they remember a certain passage (not the exact words!) for which they responded, "Praise God!" Allow each youth the opportunity to speak. Ask the youth why they considered that particular verse or sentence to be positive.

After their initial responses, read through the story again and allow the youth the opportunity to voice their opinions. They might consider these verses as positive: 12a ("signs and wonders"), 13b ("but the people held them in high esteem"), 14, 15, 16, 19, 20, 21a ("they entered the temple at daybreak and went on with their preaching"), 22, 23, 25, 28b ("you have filled Jerusalem with your teaching"), 29, 30, 31, 32, 39a ("if it is of God, you will not be able to overthrow them"), 41, and 42. The interpretations of the youth may differ from yours and from the others in the class. Be open to their reactions to the story.

Connecting to the Story (5–10 minutes)

OPTION A

Needed: pencils, "Always, Sometimes, Never" handouts
Give each youth a pencil and a copy of the "Always, Sometimes, Never" handout. Invite the youth to look at the handout with you. Explain to the youth that the handout includes eight statements. Under each statement are the words "Always,"
"Sometimes," and "Never." Ask the youth to read each statement silently and consider it, deciding how true the statement is for them personally, and then to circle one of the choices, "Always," "Sometimes," or "Never." Encourage the youth to take enough time to reflect on each statement.

When they have finished writing, go over the handout together. As you read each statement, ask the youth if they would like to share their answers. Ask a question such as "What did you think of this statement?" Some youth may wish to share their responses and explain how they have felt persecuted or how they rejoice. Other youth may be more reluctant to share this personal information. Be sensitive to the needs of the youth.

OPTION B

Needed: news magazines or Internet articles
Invite the youth to gather around a table for this activity. Place the various magazines on the table within easy reach of each of the youth. Explain that today's Bible story describes the persecution of Peter and the apostles. Ask the youth to think about the persecution of persons for their beliefs today, posing questions such as:
■ Do you think that persecution exists today?
■ Can you think of examples?
Youth might mention the persecution of Christians in China, Christians in Kosovo, Muslims in Kosovo, and so forth, or they may recall the Holocaust and the persecution of Jews. Allow the youth the opportunity to brainstorm for a few moments. Then instruct them to

look through the magazines and see if they can find articles about persecution of persons for their beliefs. Allow several moments for the youth to look through the magazines for articles.

Encourage each youth to share briefly one article with the group.

**Exploring the Story
(10–15 minutes)**
OPTION A
Needed: pencils, "Signs and Wonders" handouts, Bibles
Give the youth each a pencil and a copy of the "Signs and Wonders" handout. Invite them to look at the handout with you. Explain that today's Bible story begins with, "Now many signs and wonders were done among the people through the apostles" (verse 12). Point out that there are signs and wonders in today's passage as well as in the four preceding chapters of Acts. Instruct the youth to work with a partner, reading through those chapters to identify other signs and wonders and then writing their findings on their handouts next to the appropriate chapter.

Some of their discoveries might include: chapter 1—Jesus appears after his crucifixion, Jesus ascends into heaven; chapter 2—Pentecost (the coming of the Holy Spirit), wonders and signs by the apostles with the believers having "all things in common" (v. 44); chapter 3—Peter heals a crippled beggar; chapter 4—the council's amazement at Peter and John, the believers share their possessions; chapter 5—Ananias and Sapphira lie about the sale of property, attempt to hold out on God, and fall down dead. Today's story also describes the healing of many and the apostles' release from jail by an angel.

Allow time for the youth to complete the handout and invite them to share their discoveries.

OPTION B
Needed: pencils and paper or large index cards, Bibles, topical Bible, commentaries, Bible dictionary
Ask the youth to work in three groups for this activity. Invite the youth to explore today's story in greater detail. Point out the various resources and describe how each might be used (a topical Bible to discover related passages to specific themes, commentaries to see how others have interpreted the story, and a Bible dictionary to explore concepts).

Invite one group to make discoveries about the council or Sanhedrin that is mentioned in today's story. Who are the members? What is its purpose? Where else in the New Testament is it mentioned? Invite the second group to make discoveries about other early Christians who have been persecuted or imprisoned and protected by God. Invite the third group to make discoveries about those who have been jealous of the power of God and God's followers.

Encourage the youth to share their discoveries with the group.

**Living the Story
(5–10 minutes)**
OPTION A
Needed: strips of brightly colored construction paper, glue, pencils
Give each participant a pencil and two or three strips of brightly colored construction paper. Ask the youth to join with you in making

a prayer chain, literally! Encourage each youth to write a prayer concern on one of the strips of construction paper, and invite those who have several prayer concerns to use additional strips of the paper. Remind them to include prayers for people who may be persecuted for their faith. Remind them, too, that they may have a special joy or thanksgiving that could be noted as well.

When the youth have finished writing their individual prayers, invite them to make an old-fashioned paper chain by intertwining their circles with the others and then gluing or stapling them. Ask the participants to share their prayer concerns with the group as they glue and add each circle to the chain. Some youth may be eager to share their concerns while others might be more reluctant. Be sensitive to the needs of the individuals in the group. You might want to display the prayer chain on the wall.

When all the youth have finished, close the session in prayer, asking God to hear our prayer concerns, even those that are unwritten or unspoken.

OPTION B
Needed: pieces of ribbon that are long enough to tie around a wrist, markers
Give each participant a piece of the ribbon and a marker. Invite the youth to work with a partner for this activity. Point out that we are each a wonder of God's creation. Ask the youth to draw on the ribbon a small, simple design, such

as a star, flower, or happy face, that might symbolize being a wonder of God. Allow a moment or two for the youth to create their own symbols.

When they have completed the drawing, invite the youth to have their partners tie the ribbon around their wrist. Encourage the youth to share with their partners what they have drawn.

Whenever everyone is done with this activity, you might enjoy ending the session with a group hug.

Things to Ponder
Youth may be familiar with stories of persecution of God's people in the Bible. This session's story of Peter's and the apostles' imprisonment and flogging may seem like one more story of persecution that occurred thousands of years ago. Youth may not realize, however, that persecution of Christians still occurs today. This session may cause them to examine their own lives and evaluate the strength of their own beliefs. Youth may feel stronger admiration for those who do face persecution for their convictions.

Looking Ahead
The next session focuses on the song that Mary sang in praise of God prior to the birth of Jesus. Several of the options make use of music. Gather songs of praise to God that the youth might know and plan to play these as the youth arrive. Because this session deals with Mary's pregnancy, the subject of teen pregnancy may come up. You might want to look for news or Internet articles that deal with this subject.

"Always, Sometimes, Never"

I feel God's presence in my life.

Always   Sometimes   Never

I have felt persecuted or punished for my beliefs.

Always   Sometimes   Never

I rejoice in opportunities to serve God.

Always   Sometimes   Never

I remain faithful to my beliefs.

Always   Sometimes   Never

I praise God in my actions.

Always   Sometimes   Never

I am willing to make sacrifices for God.

Always   Sometimes   Never

I believe God takes care of me.

Always   Sometimes   Never

I obey God rather than those around me.

Always   Sometimes   Never

~~~~~~
"Signs and Wonders" Handout

There are "signs and wonders" of God's power in each of the first five chapters of Acts. Explore the Scriptures and list your discoveries.

ACTS 1:

ACTS 2:

ACTS 3:

ACTS 4:

ACTS 5:

13. My Soul Magnifies the Lord

Bible Story: Luke 1:39–56

A Story behind the Story

Throughout the Bible, God often uses ordinary people to accomplish incredible things. The story of Jesus' birth is no different. An elderly priest, an unmarried teenage girl, a simple carpenter, and a woman thought to be barren are all used to fulfill the mighty plan of redemption.

The story for this session focuses on Mary's visit to Elizabeth. Luke begins his Gospel with two separate but parallel birth announcements. The first story is the miracle of Elizabeth's pregnancy. Both Elizabeth and her husband, Zechariah, are very old. An angel announces the good news to Zechariah, and the faithful priest can hardly believe it. Because of his doubt, he is silenced until the good news is fulfilled. After the announcement to Zechariah, the angel Gabriel visits Mary and tells her that she will give birth to Jesus.

The two seemingly separate stories come together when the women meet—Mary goes to visit Elizabeth. When Mary enters the home and greets Elizabeth, Elizabeth's child leaps for joy within her womb and signals that Mary has indeed been blessed. The infant John, soon to be born, has already begun his work to prepare the way for the Lord. Elizabeth is filled with the Spirit, which sets the stage for her prophetic announcements about Mary. All that happens between these women fulfills the announcements that were made to Zechariah. Elizabeth proclaims that Mary will be the mother of her Lord and offers her blessing for Mary's faithfulness to God's word.

Elizabeth's declarations are matched by the song of praise offered by Mary. This song is often called *The Magnificat*. Mary declares her praise of God for what God has done for her and for the world. She speaks of God's redeeming work in the world not as a future event but as something that has already been fulfilled. Her song foreshadows the ministry of Jesus to the least and the lost. The Magnificat makes clear the pattern for God's activity to save the world: send a Savior who will call people to repentance, forgive sinners, lift up the lowly, heal the sick, cast out demons, eat with outcasts, and die a redemptive death.

Enter the Story

What comes to your mind when you hear the word *announcement*? Your mind may wander to your homeroom class in school and the announcements you heard over the PA system, or to graduation or birth announcements, or perhaps to the announcements at a football game. In all of these situations, announcements are made because someone wants to share information with others. That is what our story for this week is all about. It is the birth announcement for our Lord.

Find a place where you can spend a few minutes with the text. Read through the exchange between Mary and Elizabeth in

Section Four

〰〰〰

Liberation/ Justice

by Kissa Hamilton

- **How can I praise God when life is difficult?**
- **With whom could I share exciting news?**
- **Could God use me to do something incredible?**
- **What's my song? How and when shall I sing it?**
- **How should society respond to teenage pregnancy?**
- **How does the birth of Jesus affect me?**

YOU MAY NEED

- **pencils and paper**
- **index cards**
- **tapes or CDs (preferably music that youth often listen to)**
- **portable stereo**
- **candy or prizes**
- **"Singing My Song to God" handouts**
- **"Ups and Downs" handouts**
- **Bibles**
- **Bible study materials (concordance, commentary on Luke, and others)**
- **map showing location of Nazareth and Judean hill country (optional)**
- **candle**
- **matches**
- **video camera (optional)**

Luke 1:39–45. What might God be trying to announce to you in this story? What announcements might God want the youth in your class to hear from this story? Then read Mary's song in Luke 1:46–56. Take a few minutes to pray that the youth in your care might see Christ announced in you and in their lives in a new way.

Setting the Stage (5–10 minutes)

As you prepare for the group to hear Mary's song, have music playing as the youth arrive. Check in with the group to find out how school is going and how their week was. Ask the group to answer a funny question like, "If you could be any musical instrument, what would you be and why?" Then do one of the following musical activities.

OPTION A

Needed: paper or index cards and pencils

Distribute pencils and paper. Ask the participants to write their names on the paper, along with their favorite song and a song that says something about the kind of person they are. Tell them to make sure that no one else sees their responses. When they are finished writing, ask them to hand in their responses to you. Mix up the papers and read the responses randomly, asking group members to try to identify the person who wrote each response. After everyone has guessed, reveal the identities of the people who wrote the responses, and allow them to explain why they chose the particular songs they did.

OPTION B

Needed: tapes/CDs, portable stereo, candy or small gifts for prizes

Play a few rounds of Name That Tune. If possible, bring some tapes or CDs and a portable stereo. If you do not have a portable stereo, ask for a volunteer to select a song and prepare to sing or hum it. Ask for two contestants to begin the activity. The two will bid on how many seconds they will need to listen to the music to be able to "name that tune." Begin the bidding with two minutes and have the first player respond with "I can name that tune in _____ minutes/seconds." The next player responds with a lesser amount of time. Bidding alternates until one player feels that he or she cannot go any further and says to the opponent, "Name that tune." The music is played or hummed for the designated amount of time, and the player has ten seconds to name the tune. If the contestant can name the tune, then he or she is the winner. If not, the challenger wins. Award candy or small gifts as prizes.

Telling the Story (5–10 minutes)

OPTION A

Needed: Bibles, paper, pencils

Explain to the group that your story for today features two main characters, Mary and Elizabeth. Form two groups. Ask one group to tell you what they already know about Mary. Ask the other group to tell you what they already know about Elizabeth. Reassure youth that it is okay if they do not remember who these people are. Then explain that you or a volunteer will read a story about a time when these two people met. Invite the Mary group to stand whenever you mention Mary, and invite the Elizabeth group to stand whenever you mention Elizabeth. Practice a few times before you begin reading. Then read or have volunteers read Luke 1:39–56, reminding the appropriate group to stand whenever its character is mentioned.

After reading the story, distribute Bibles, paper, and pencils to each group. Ask the Elizabeth group to work together to write in their own words what Elizabeth says to Mary. Ask the Mary group to work together to write in their own words the song that Mary sings to God. Allow a few minutes for groups to finish their summaries, and then invite the groups to share their summaries out loud.

OPTION B
Needed: Bibles, paper, pencils
Distribute paper and pencils to the youth. Before reading the story, ask them to think of reasons people might have for praising God. Talk together briefly about some of the those reasons. Then explain to the participants that they are about to hear a story from the Bible in which two people give many different reasons for offering praise to God. Ask them to listen carefully to the story and write down the reasons these two people give for praising or blessing God. Read or invite volunteers to read Luke 1:39–56 slowly, pausing as needed to allow the participants time to write. Then distribute Bibles to the youth and invite them to find Luke 1:39–56. Allow time for them to look at the text for

themselves to find other reasons that Mary and Elizabeth give for offering praise to God.

Reacting to the Story (5–10 minutes)
OPTION A
Needed: paper or index cards, pencils
In the story, Mary immediately knows that she wants to share her exciting news with her friend and relative Elizabeth. When friends spend time together, they usually ask each other questions to find out how their lives have been since they last spoke or were together. Invite the youth to find a partner. Give each person an index card and a pencil. Ask the participants to write on the card one question that they think Elizabeth would want to ask Mary. After they have had time to formulate a question, invite them to ask their partners their questions. First, one partner should take on the role of Mary and try to respond to the other's question the way he or she believes Mary would answer. Then the pairs should switch roles. After everyone has finished, gather the group together and have each person read aloud his or her question for Mary and briefly tell what the partner's response to the question was. Invite other youth to share how they think Mary would have responded to that question.

OPTION B
Needed: Bibles, pencils, paper
Form small groups and invite the youth to find Luke 1:39–46. In the story, Elizabeth and Mary mention several reasons they have for praising God: the blessing of Elizabeth's

pregnancy, the good news that God is saving people through Mary's child, and so on. Ask the youth to read between the lines in these verses and consider other reasons that Elizabeth and Mary could have had for praising God. Suggest that other things that may have been happening around them, other blessings from God that may not be explained in this story but likely were present in their lives. Encourage the youth to work with others in their small group to read the verses that precede this passage to get a better idea of the context of the story. Allow about five minutes for discussion. Then have the youth share their responses with the larger group. Then ask each youth to write on an index card the one reason for praising God in this story that seems most significant or important to him or her.

**Connecting to the Story
(5–10 minutes)**
OPTION A
Mary was excited about the news that she had to share with Elizabeth, but she also was faced with some difficulties because of her news. Form small groups, if needed, and invite the youth to talk together about Mary's difficulties. The youth may mention teenage pregnancy, ridicule from others, exclusion from friends and family, fear that no one would believe her story, concern about what would happen to her and her child, and so forth. After considering several difficulties, ask the youth, "How are the difficulties that Mary faced like the difficulties that you have to face today?" Allow time for the youth who wish

to do so to share their responses and talk about these issues. Listen and give them a chance to really share their struggles. After they have had time to share, remind them that in spite of all the difficulties that were present for Mary, she still found a way to praise God in her song. Ask the students, "Is praising God hard or easy when your life is challenging? Why? What are some ways that you might praise God in the midst of your own difficulties?"

OPTION B
Needed: pencils, "Singing My Song to God" handouts
Give each participant a copy of the "Singing My Song to God" handout. This activity can be done in small groups, in pairs, or individually. Choose what will work best with the group. Tell the youth that they are going to create a contemporary "song" to God, because just as Mary voiced a song of praise to God in our story, we should be people who praise God for the ways we have been blessed. Ask the participants to spend some time either alone or with their groups creating a poem, song, or rap praising God. Let them know that the song or poem should reflect their own personal blessings from God and does not have to be similar to Mary's song at all. Their creation should be about them and how they would tell others about what God has been doing in their lives. Remind them to use language that they would normally use and to remember that the focus is on praising God, not on glorifying ourselves. Allow five to ten minutes for the

youth to complete their work. Do not have the youth share their creations here, but choose that option under "Living the Story."

Exploring the Story
(10–15 minutes)
OPTION A
Needed: pencils, "Ups and Downs" handouts, Bibles, map showing the location of Nazareth and the Judean hill country (if available)
Give each student a pencil and a copy of the "Ups and Downs" handout. If you have a map, point out the location of Nazareth (west of the Sea of Galilee) and tell the youth that this is where Mary was when she heard that she would give birth to Jesus. Then point to the hill country of Judea, near Jerusalem. Explain that Mary traveled up and down many hills to get to Elizabeth. Likewise, both Mary and Elizabeth went through some high and low points in their lives. Ask the participants to use the handout to mark some of the high and low points for Mary, Elizabeth, and themselves. After everyone has completed the handout, talk with the youth about how they interpreted high and low points. Be prepared for the fact that some may have interpreted things differently than others.

OPTION B
Needed: Bibles, Bible study resources like Bible dictionaries or encyclopedias
Tell the youth that more women are depicted in the Book of Luke than in any of the other Gospels. One of Luke's techniques is to pair stories about men with stories about women. Invite the youth to look through the Book of Luke to find some of these pairings. One example is the story of the man who finds his lost sheep and the woman who finds her lost coin in Luke 15:4–10. Another is the list of the male followers of Jesus in Luke 6:12–19 and the list of females in Luke 8:1–3. See how many the participants can locate. While some youth are looking for stories about women in Luke's Gospel, invite a few others to use the Bible study materials to discover the role of women in Jesus' day. Suggest they look up "women" in a Bible dictionary or encyclopedia or look for references to women in other Gospels. When all of the groups have finished their research, invite the group who studied the role of women to share their findings first. Then ask the other groups to talk about the stories of women included in Luke's Gospel. Discuss the following questions:
■ How did Jesus treat women?
■ Why is it important that Luke includes so many women in this Gospel?
■ What does this tell you about the story about Elizabeth and Mary?

Living the Story
(5–10 minutes)
OPTION A
Needed: large candle, matches
Gather the group together in a circle for a closing time together. Light a large candle and place it in the center of the circle. Lower the lights, if possible, to create a different mood for the more serious closing time. Ask the youth to respond to the question, "How were you surprised by the story?" Give them a few

minutes to answer. Then ask, "What does this story have to say to you in your daily life?" Give them a few minutes to answer this question. Thank all the students for their hard work during class. Be sure that each person gets some special recognition for his or her contributions. Take any prayer requests that the group might have. Then either you or a volunteer can close the time in prayer. Pray that each of you will have the wisdom to know how to praise God in the midst of any difficulties that you might encounter.

OPTION B

If you chose Option B under "Connecting to the Story" above, you may want to use the following exercise for this segment.

Needed: songs, poems, or raps written by the youth during "Connecting to the Story," Option B, video camera (optional)

Invite the group to share their creative work on the poems, songs, and raps that they created earlier. Ask for a volunteer to share first. Do not force anyone to share who isn't comfortable. You may want to record the performances with a video camera so that the youth and parents can watch them together. After the performances, gather the group together in a circle for a closing time. Light a large candle and place it in the center of the circle. Lower the lights, if possible, to create a different mood. Thank all the students for their hard work. Be sure that each person gets some special recognition for his or her contributions. Take any prayer requests that the group might have. Then either you or a volunteer can close the group in prayer, asking God to show all of you how to offer praise in the midst of any difficulties that you might encounter.

Things to Ponder

The discussion about Mary may lead to a discussion of teenage pregnancy, sex before marriage, and abortion. The youth may have a classmate who became pregnant, or they may have had that experience themselves. Do not be afraid of talking honestly and openly about these topics. You might want to be prepared with some extra information about them should they come up in class.

Looking Ahead

The next session looks at the prophecy in Isaiah that Christians believe points toward Jesus. You might want to learn a little about Old Testament prophecy since many of the students will not know about it at all. Be prepared for questions about false prophets who have come forward in the past few years. Students may want to discuss how we can tell a false prophet from a real one.

Singing My Song to God

Take a few minutes to think about your own reasons for praising God. Then write your own "song." You may want to create a poem, song, or rap praising God. It should reflect your own personal blessings from God and does not have to be the similar to Mary's song at all. Be sure to use language that you would normally use, and remember that the focus is on praising God, not on glorifying yourself.

Ups and Downs

When Mary learned that she was pregnant, she set out to visit Elizabeth "in the hill country" (Luke 1:39). Mary and Elizabeth certainly had a lot of ups and downs. Explore Luke 1 and 2 to identify some of their high points and some of their low points.

Mary

Elizabeth

Me

14. Light to Those in Darkness

Bible Story: Isaiah 9:1–7

A Story behind the Story

Isaiah lived in the southern kingdom of Judah in the eighth century B.C. and watched with horror as the northern kingdom of Israel was conquered by Assyria. This prophet believed that a similar fate awaited Judah. Isaiah believed that the people deserved to suffer because of their lack of faithfulness to God, but he also believed that God would provide salvation. The light of hope would shine in the midst of darkness, and it would come in the form of a child.

Children play an important role in Isaiah's prophecies. His first child's name means "A remnant shall return." In Isaiah 7:1–9, Isaiah goes with this son to meet Ahaz, king of Judah. He tries to convince the king not to join forces with foreign nations but rather to rely on God to defend the nation. The name of Isaiah's son is intended to provide a message of hope. King Ahaz hesitates to rely on God, so Isaiah offers another message through the name of another child—Immanuel. He tells Ahaz that a young woman (or a virgin) will soon have a son named Immanuel and that before the child is old enough to eat solid food, the northern kingdom of Israel will fall. The prophet then mentions a child that his wife will soon bear (8:1–4). The name of this child means "The spoil speeds, the prey hastens." Before this child learns to speak, Assyria will triumph over Israel. Isaiah 8:18 explains that the prophet and his children are "signs and portents in Israel from the LORD of hosts." These children are a warning that the nation of Judah must hope in God and not form alliances with other nations, but King Ahaz and the nation ignore Isaiah's message. Therefore, Isaiah predicts that "they will look to the earth, but will see only distress and darkness" (8:22).

Suddenly out of the darkness comes a ray of light that floods the land with joyful singing of freedom. Isaiah declares, "The people who walked in darkness have seen a great light" (9:2). And this hope comes because of the birth of a new child—not a child of warning and judgment, but a child of hope and promise. Isaiah believed that this child would be an earthly king, but Christians see this child as Jesus, born among us to bring light to all who live in darkness.

Enter the Story

Hope is a experience that many people do not have. They live in a world that echoes with hopelessness. Take a few moments to consider situations in the lives of youth or in your community that seem hopeless. Think about what it is like to live with this kind of despair.

Now read Isaiah 9:1–7. What does this prophet say to people who live without hope? Where can hope be found? This story speaks of hope—hope that things will be better, hope that God is not done working in our world, hope that the light will shine in our world once again. Read the passage

POSSIBLE YOUTH CONTACT POINTS

- Why hope in God?
- What is God doing in our world today?
- Where is the "light"?
- Who is living in despair and darkness?
- How can the light of Christ help?
- Where is the endless peace that was promised?
- Who are modern-day prophets? What is their message?

YOU MAY NEED

- newsprint, markers
- Bibles
- flashlight
- large candle
- small candles for youth
- matches
- photocopies of Isaiah 9:1–7
- paper, pencils
- construction paper, scissors, glue, magazines
- Bible study resources (Bible maps or atlas, Bible dictionary, biblical concordance or commentaries)
- "Would You Name Your Kid . . ." handouts
- "My Own Prophecy" handouts

again, and try to think of places or situations in which this kind of hope is present.

Pray for hope for your youth. If you know of special needs in their lives, pray for those needs as well. And pray for yourself, that you might have hope and share it freely.

Setting the Stage (10–15 minutes)

Check in with the group as they enter your meeting space. Ask them how school is going and how their week was. Check up on any prayer concerns that they may have mentioned in the past. Then have the group answer an odd question such as, "Have you ever been scared of the dark? If so, when? And what was it like?" Encourage them to think about recent experiences, such as a time when they might have been lost in a dark place, as well as experiences from early childhood.

OPTION A

Needed: newsprint, markers

Post newsprint on the wall and ask the group the following question, "What is your definition of 'important'?" Explain that there are no right or wrong answers. After receiving a few responses to this question, write on the newsprint: "Top ten signs something important is going to happen . . ." Invite the group to offer suggestions, but do not try to rank them in order at this time. If your group is large, consider forming smaller groups of four to six. When you have ten items on the list, work together to rank them with the least important as number ten moving to the most important as number one. After completing the ranked list, have one of the

youth read it off in his or her best talk show voice. Be sure to include a drum roll before number one.

OPTION B

Have the group come up with their own infomercial selling "light" to people who have spent years in the darkness. If you have a very large group, you may want to break it down into smaller groups for this activity. Encourage the groups to work together to promote the product. Everyone should have a part. Suggest that the groups consider offering personal testimonies about how great the light is and why others might want to have it as well. Encourage them to consider listing all the positive qualities of the light and the things that the light can do for them. Tell them they might also depict someone actually receiving the light and being totally transformed by it right there on the infomercial. Remind them that one of the best selling points for this light, of course, is that it comes completely assembled and it is free. Encourage creativity. Allow 5–10 minutes for preparation. Then ask groups to share their infomercials.

Telling the Story (5 minutes)

OPTION A

Needed: Bibles, flashlight (if needed)

Gather the group together in a circle. Distribute Bibles, and help the youth find Isaiah 9:1–7. Ask for volunteers to take turns reading the verses in this passage. Encourage them to read slowly and carefully with a majestic feeling. Lower the lights or close curtains in the room to make the room as dark as possible. Give the flashlight to the readers (if needed). Stand near the light switch or near a window as the youth read the beginning of the story. (Note: You may wish to read verse one because there are many names in that verse that are difficult to pronounce.) When the words from verse 2b are read, "The people who walked in darkness have seen a great light," turn on all the lights or throw open a curtain to allow light to come into the room. Then have the volunteers continue reading their parts in order to finish out the Scripture.

OPTION B

Needed: large candle, candle for each youth, matches, at least seven photocopies of the same translation of Isaiah 9:1–7

Gather the group together around a table. In the center of the table, light a large candle and place one small candle for each youth around it. If possible, dim the lights in the room. Distribute copies of Isaiah 9:1–7 or Bibles. This passage has seven verses, so form seven groups to read the passage, keeping in mind that it is okay to have only one person in a group. If you cannot form seven groups, you may have one group read more than one verse. Explain that Group 1 will read verse one. Then members of Group 1 light their individual candles. Then Groups 1 and 2 will read verse two, and members of Group 2 will light their individual candles. Then, Groups 1, 2, and 3 will read verse three, and so on. The idea is that the voices and the lights will become stronger as the reading continues. Keep going around the circle until everyone in the group reads

the last verse and all the small candles have been lit.

Reacting to the Story
(5–10 minutes)

OPTION A

Needed: Bible, newsprint, markers

Ask the youth to close their eyes and try to picture the Bible story in their minds as you read it. Read Isaiah 9:1–7 aloud slowly. After they have heard the story again, ask them to name all the images or pictures that came to mind when they heard this story. List their responses on a piece of newsprint. Encourage the participants to describe the images that they saw, not repeat words they heard from the text. Explain that this exercise is about visualization, and there may not necessarily be a clear connection between the picture in their mind's eye and the words they heard. Talk together about these images, using the following questions:

■ Which mental image/picture meant the most to you?
■ Why was that image the most important?
■ What spoke to you most in this story?
■ What do you think God might be trying to say to you through this Scripture?

After you have discussed the images that came from the text, ask the youth what questions they have about the text. Write their questions on newsprint.

OPTION B

Needed: Bible

Tell the youth that they are going to hear the Scripture read again but this time you want them to participate in melodrama. Explain that in an old-

fashioned melodrama, the characters overemphasize their actions to reveal their personal reactions to what is happening. For example, when you read about doom and darkness, youth might walk around with their shoulders slumped like they are depressed. When the light comes to them, they might look startled and blinded as if they were looking into a bright light. The youth will need to have plenty of room to react to the words they hear, so be sure to get them up and moving. Read the Scripture slowly, pausing often to give them a chance to react to what you are saying. After the melodrama has been enacted, ask the group the following questions:
■ What was easiest for you to react to?
■ What was the hardest for you to react to?
■ What spoke to you the most in this story?
■ What do you think God might be trying to say to you through this Scripture?

Connecting to the Story (10–15 minutes)

OPTION A

Needed: paper, pencils
If you have more than six youth, have the group form several small groups. If your group has fewer than six youth, have them work in pairs. Assign each group a section of the Scripture and instruct them to rewrite it in their own words. Explain that they should try to capture the main message of the section, but they do not have to use the same words or form as the original story. After the groups have had time to work, gather the group together and read the sections in the proper sequence, to hear the whole prophecy in modern words. Follow this with a discussion about the Scripture, asking questions such as:
■ Did we capture the meaning of the original story in the one written in our own words?
■ What expectations would you have if you heard this message proclaimed today?
■ What did you understand for the first time after writing your own version?

OPTION B

Needed: construction paper, scissors, magazines, glue
Distribute construction paper, scissors, glue, and magazines. Ask each youth to cut pictures and words out of the magazines and then glue them onto the piece of construction paper, creating a collage that depicts their reaction to the Scripture story. Explain that the collage can represent the pictures that came to their minds or the emotions they felt when they heard the story. Let them know that if they cannot find a picture of a specific image or an exact word, they can draw their own picture or write the word themselves. After the group has had time to create their collages, gather the group back together. Ask for a few volunteers to talk about what they put on their collages and what they mean to them. After everyone who wants to share has had a chance, ask the group questions such as:
■ Did your collage capture the meaning of the story?
■ If you heard this message proclaimed today, what would you expect to happen?
■ How do you understand the story differently than you did before?

**Exploring the Story
(10–15 minutes)**

OPTION A

Needed: Bibles, Bible study resources like Bible dictionaries and commentaries, pencils, "Would You Name Your Kid . . ." handouts

Ask the youth if they have ever heard preachers or speakers tell stories about children as a way of illustrating a point. Invite the youth to share such stories or to recall such speakers. Explain that the prophet Isaiah often referred to children in the messages God gave him to deliver to the people; these children were like sermon illustrations for Isaiah.

Form groups of two to four. Distribute "Would You Name Your Kid . . ." handouts, as well as Bibles and pencils. Invite the groups to use the handout to discover the significance of some of the children mentioned in Isaiah. If they have questions that they have difficulty answering with the text, encourage them to look for the answers in Bible study resources. After about ten minutes, talk together about their findings. Ask questions such as:

■ How would you like to have the name of one of Isaiah's children?

■ Did these children bring good or bad news?

■ What was significant about each child?

■ Why would Isaiah talk about children in this way?

OPTION B

Needed: Bibles, Bible atlas or maps, Bible dictionary, commentaries on Isaiah, paper, pencils

Isaiah 9:1 includes the names of countries; it is easy to read these words and miss their significance.

Form three groups. Give Bibles, pencils, and paper to all groups. Ask one group to find information about Zebulun, another to find information about Naphtali, and the third to find information about Galilee. Ask each group to answer these questions: Where was this place? Who lived there when Isaiah was preaching? Why did this place need light?

Help the youth discover that Zebulun and Naphtali were two of the tribes of Israel. They were located in the northern part of Israel, and Naphtali was among the first to be conquered by Assyria (see 2 Kings 15:29). This entire northern region was sometimes called Galilee. Because these places were farther away from the rest of the nation, the people there were more susceptible to foreign influence.

Invite the groups to share their discoveries.

Ask the youth to find Matthew 4:12–16 and have a volunteer read this passage aloud. Talk together about why Jesus quoted these verses when he began his public ministry. Ask: What does this mean?

**Living the Story
(5–10 minutes)**

OPTION A

Needed: large candle, paper, pencils

Gather the group together in a circle for a closing time together. Light a large candle and place it in the center of the circle. If possible, you might want to lower the lights to create a different mood for the more serious closing time. Leave enough light so that the youth will be able to see well enough to write. Remind the group that Christians believe that Isaiah's vision has been fulfilled in Jesus; he is our Wonderful Counselor, Mighty God, Everlasting Father, and Prince of Peace. Give sheets of paper to the youth and ask them to fold the paper twice so that there are four quadrants. Invite the youth to write prayers in each quadrant: in one, a prayer about a situation in which they need a Wonderful Counselor; in another, a prayer about a situation in which they need a Mighty God; in another, a prayer to the Everlasting Father; in the fourth, a prayer to the Prince of Peace about a situation where peace is needed. After youth have had time to write, invite those who are willing to read one or more of their prayers aloud. After they have read, invite the other youth to say these words from Isaiah 9:7 aloud: "The zeal of the LORD of hosts will do this."

OPTION B
Needed: "My Own Prophecy" handouts
Gather the group together in a circle for a closing time together. Thank all the youth for their hard work during class. Try to make sure that each person gets some special recognition for his or her contributions. Talk together about what a prophet is and what a prophet does. Then tell the youth that it is their turn to be a prophet like Isaiah. Give each person a copy of the "My Own Prophecy" handout. Ask the youth to write a short prophecy of hope for their own future, trying to see their future as God sees it. When most youth have finished writing, ask volunteers to share what they have written. Then talk together about any prayer requests that the group might have. Invite a volunteer to close with prayer, or offer a prayer yourself, asking God to give all of you hope for the future.

Things to Ponder
Many youth may not understand what a prophet is. Prophets are men and women whom God uses to bring a message to God's people. Prophets appear throughout the Bible and continue even today. Often they are unwelcome because of the difficult messages they bring. Some people who claim to be prophets are false prophets. You might talk together about how to tell the difference between false and real prophets. Encourage the youth to use Scripture and teachings from the church plus a good dose of common sense to determine whether a person is truly bringing a message from God.

Looking Ahead
The next session will look at the birth of Jesus as described in Luke's Gospel. One of the options invites youth to create a life-sized nativity scene. If you choose that option, allow yourself time to gather the materials you will need. "Setting the Stage," Option B, asks youth to describe how their family prepares for the birth of Jesus. If you plan to use this option, you might want to inform youth so that they can talk with parents or grandparents about their family traditions before the next session.

Would You Name Your Kid...?

Isaiah's children had strange names like Shear-jashub or Maher-shalal-hash-baz, but the names had significant meanings. Look up these verses, which explain why Isaiah chose these names.

Isaiah 7:3–9
What is the significance of this name?

Isaiah 8:1–4
What is the significance of this name?

Isaiah also speaks of another child who will soon be born to a young woman. Read **Isaiah 7:10–17** to discover the name of this child and what the name means.

Isaiah 9:6 tells of another child. What are the names for this child? What is different about this child?

My Own Prophecy

Prophets are people who deliver messages from God. Today, you get to be the prophet! Write a short prophecy of hope for your own future. What will God do in your life? How will God use you? What warnings does God have for you? Write whatever you think God wants to say to you.

15. You Will Find a Child

Bible Story: Luke 2:1–20

A Story behind the Story

Finally, we arrive at the birth of the Savior. After a long chapter describing the annunciations of the two births, the meeting of Mary and Elizabeth, and the events surrounding the birth and naming of John, the birth of Jesus is reported with a minimum of detail in Luke's Gospel. The first five verses of the second chapter set the scene for Jesus' birth, and the next two simple verses describe how Jesus was born. The following eleven verses record the angelic announcement to the shepherds and their visit to the Christ Child. The structure of this text indicates that Luke's purpose is to show the significance of the birth in relation to world history but that the important part of this story is the faithfulness of the shepherds.

Why does Luke spend so many verses telling us about where Jesus was born? The context of Jesus' birth has thematic and theological significance. Jesus, the son of David, the bringer of peace, was born in Bethlehem, the city of David, as foretold by the prophets. The Savior of all people was born under the reign of Caesar Augustus, whose peace paled before that announced by the angels. The Messiah born under Roman oppression, which was made painfully evident in the forced registration, would overthrow the powerful and raise up the oppressed. The context of Jesus' birth is itself a commentary on his future role. It is a sign of who and what Jesus would be in this world.

The story of Jesus' birth is filled with surprise. Angels caught people off guard to announce the news, but their message was even more surprising than their presence. God chose to enter into human history as a helpless newborn child. As this child, God was laid in a rough feeding trough. Imagine the kind of splendor that God could have chosen, but instead God slipped unobtrusively into a small town far from the powers of the world, born to a poor young couple. No elaborate preparations were made for the birth. The first visitors were not kings but simple shepherds. By entering into the world in this way, God was announcing that a new kingdom was being established in which God would identify with the powerless, the oppressed, the poor, and the homeless. Entering into this new kingdom requires that we come with a humility and a deep need to be loved by this surprising, out-of-the-ordinary God.

Enter the Story

Bethlehem is the place God came to us through the birth of a child. It is a place of mystery and wonder, far removed from the ordinary world in which we live. Angels populate the skies and may appear at any time to shepherds in the fields. Far from the problems of the world, the mother and father hover over their firstborn child lying in a manger. This child will be the Messiah, the

- What does the way in which Jesus entered the world tell us about who Jesus was?
- Why did God choose this way for Jesus to be born?
- How does the way that Jesus entered the world affect my understanding of him?
- What does the birth of Jesus tell me about God?
- What is important to me?
- What is important to God?

YOU MAY NEED

- material for life-size Nativity, such as fabric, old bathrobes, halos, hay
- Christmas music and tape/CD player
- Christmas snacks
- "The Best Christmas Ever" handouts
- pencils
- Bibles
- *A Charlie Brown Christmas* video
- TV/VCR
- contemporary translation of the Bible
- newsprint
- markers
- "www.birthofchrist.com" handouts
- markers or crayons for youth
- paper
- parallel Bible or *Gospel Parallels* (optional)
- Bible study materials, such as Bible commentaries, maps, Bible dictionary
- art supplies, such as construction paper, scissors, glue, glitter, stickers
- small notebook or journal for each youth (to be used again in the next session)

Savior for all the earth. This story has a real fairy-tale quality to it. We long to leave the maddening world of the holiday season and enter into this simple, quiet story where we can feel the wonder of God's grace.

And yet, Bethlehem was a crowded city, filled with hurried, frightened travelers who were concerned about taxes and the government. The people who gathered there were under a great deal of stress. God chose to enter this frightened and worried world through the simple birth of a child.

As you prepare to read this story from Luke 2:1–20, lay your cares and concerns before God, and invite the Christ Child to be born anew in your life.

Setting the Stage (5–15 minutes)

OPTION A

Needed: material for life-size Nativity, such as fabric, old bathrobes, halos, hay

Work with the youth to create a life-size manger scene in your meeting space. Costume and prop suggestions include: fabric or old bathrobes for shepherds, fabric for people to drape around their heads, ears cut out of cardboard and covered with cotton on headbands for the sheep, halos and white sheets for angels, candy canes for shepherds' crooks, a doll wrapped in cloth, stuffed animals to use as barn animals, and a large star. As the youth enter the room, invite each person to become part of the story by putting on a costume or adding a prop to the scene. Be as creative as you can be and make sure that each youth has some part in the

story. You will need several shepherds and angels, but you may also double-cast the scene and have more than one Mary or Joseph. You may want to sprinkle some hay to create a barn-like atmosphere. Think about having a feeding trough for the baby and playing some Christmas music. Have fun with this activity, and try to help the youth experience what the birth of Jesus might have been like for Mary and Joseph.

OPTION B

Needed: portable stereo and CDs or tapes of Christmas music, Christmas snacks, "The Best Christmas Ever" handouts, pencils

As the youth enter the room have Christmas music playing in the background. Share some Christmas snacks with the group. You might want to share a tradition from your family, such as special Christmas cookies or your secret recipe for hot chocolate. Make the room as inviting as you can. After everyone has arrived, give each youth a pencil and a copy of "The Best Christmas Ever" handout. Allow a few minutes for the youth to complete the handouts. Then talk together about what they have written. After discussing the handouts, or when everyone is talking comfortably, ask, "How does your family prepare for Christmas?" They might answer with stories about decorating their home, shopping for presents, wrapping gifts, and so forth. Then ask, "How does your family prepare for the birth of Jesus? How is that similar to or different from your preparations for Christmas?"

Telling the Story
(10–15 minutes)
OPTION A

Needed: Bibles

Gather the youth together in a circle. Invite the group to tell the story of the birth of Jesus from Luke 2:1–20 without using their Bibles. Ask them to pretend that they are telling this story to a group of six-year-olds who have never heard it before and that they should tell it in a simple way so that it will be easily understood. Explain that they should work together to retell the story from their collective memories. Begin by giving them the first sentence of the story and then ask the youth to move on from there. Start with the youth whose birthday is closest to Christmas day. Go around the circle and ask each youth to add a phrase or sentence until the story has been completed. Encourage everyone to participate in some way. Give hints to those who may not be familiar with the story. After the group has finished, ask one or several of the youth to read the actual text from Luke 2:1–20.

OPTION B

Needed: **A Charlie Brown Christmas** *video, contemporary translation of the Bible*

One of the best ways for youth to hear the biblical story is from their own familiar culture. For this option you will need to rent or buy the Peanuts cartoon *A Charlie Brown Christmas*. Prior to the session, cue the tape to the scene at the end of the show in which Charlie Brown is trying to determine the real meaning of Christmas. Linus

steps onstage and recites a selection from Luke 2. Gather the youth around the television and show this scene. Many of them will have seen the show, but they might be surprised that the Scripture lesson for their class is right there in a cartoon they have seen before. After viewing the scene, have someone read the text from Luke 2:1–20 from a modern version of Scripture such as *The Message* or the Contemporary English Version. If your church does not have a license to show videos, ask the youth if they have seen the movie and talk together about this scene. Read Luke 2:1–20 from a traditional version such as the King James Version, and then read it from a contemporary version.

Reacting to the Story
(5–10 minutes)
OPTION A

Needed: newsprint, marker, Bibles

This option may be used following either option from "Telling the Story." This exercise is designed to invite the youth to notice differences in the ways the Christmas story is told. Post a large piece of newsprint on the wall. Give one of the youth a marker and ask him or her to be the scribe for the group.

If you chose Option A from "Telling the Story" above, ask the group to make the following three lists:

1. all the things that they left out of their story that actually appear in the biblical story
2. all the things they added that are not in the actual text
3. any other changes that they might note

If you chose Option B from "Telling the Story" above, ask the group to list all the similarities and differences between the way they heard the story from Linus and the contemporary version they heard.

Have the youth call out answers while they brainstorm together, and have the scribe write their answers on the newsprint. After the youth finish their brainstorming, add any other differences between versions that you noticed. Ask the youth to respond to these questions:
- Why is it important to see these differences?
- Why do we remember some details of this story differently?
- How do we get confused about a simple story?

OPTION B

Needed: "www.birthofchrist.com" handouts, markers or crayons
Give a marker or crayon and a copy of the "www.birthofchrist .com" handout to the youth. Invite them to work individually or in small groups to design a website that announces the birth of Jesus to cyberspace. Ask them to think about the parts of the story that are most important to them and to arrange the website so that these aspects of the story get the most emphasis. Explain that they may include in the website any information about Jesus' birth that they think is important—pictures of the manger or the happy family, interviews with shepherds, and so on. They may also create links to other websites, such as www.CaesarAugustus.com or www.Bethlehem.com. Allow 5–10 minutes to create websites. Then invite youth who are willing to share what they have created with the rest of the group.

Connecting to the Story (10 minutes)
OPTION A

Needed: paper, pencils
This activity invites youth to imagine what would happen if the host of angels who announced the news of Jesus' birth to shepherds were to announce the same news today. Distribute paper and pencil. The youth may work in small groups or individually on this project. Assign each group or individual one of the following locations (or make up your own):
- church
- school cafeteria
- mall
- neighborhood
- football game
- beach
- fast food restaurant
- highway
- youth center
- hospital
- jail

Ask groups to write or prepare to tell what they think would happen if the angels came to that location with the news of Jesus' birth. Encourage them to consider the following questions:
- How would the angels get the attention of the people there?
- What would the angels say?
- How would people respond?
- What would happen next?

After all the groups have had a chance to share what they think would happen in their respective locations, invite the youth to talk together about how they think they would respond to this news.

OPTION B

Needed: "www.birthofchrist.com" handouts, markers or crayons

If you have not already done so, give each youth a copy of the handout and explain that this is a website announcing the birth of Christ. If you used Option B under "Reacting to the Story," the youth will have designed websites explaining the story of the birth of Jesus already. Invite youth to turn their handouts over and write on the back. Explain that they are creating a link to their original website. If you did not use that option, use the printed side of the handout.

Ask the youth to post a website that explains why the birth of Jesus is important to them. Encourage the youth to reflect on the significance of this story for their lives. Encourage them to consider questions such as:

■ Why was Jesus born in a barn? What does that mean to me?
■ What difference does Jesus make in my life?
■ Why am I glad that Jesus was born?
■ How do I feel about the way the shepherds responded to the birth of Jesus?
■ Do I respond to Jesus in this same way?

Allow 5–10 minutes for youth to work on this project. Then invite youth who are willing to do so to share what they have written.

Exploring the Story (10 minutes)

OPTION A

Needed: Bibles, parallel Bible or Gospel Parallels (optional)

Have the youth look at the differences between the two scriptural accounts of Jesus' birth. This lesson has been based upon Luke 2:1–20, but there is also a birth narrative found in Matthew 1:18–2:12. Divide the youth into small groups and instruct them to read both passages. If you have access to a parallel Bible or book like *Gospel Parallels: A Comparison of the Synoptic Gospels,* 5th edition, edited by Burton H. Throckmorton (Nashville: Thomas Nelson, 1993), that lists the stories next to each other, encourage the participants to look at the stories written side by side. Ask them to create a list of what is different and what is the same in these two accounts. Tell the youth to consider questions such as:

■ What things did the writers include that are the same?
■ What things did the writers include that are different?
■ What purpose would there be for each writer to include certain things?
■ What could account for the radical differences in the two stories?

It will be interesting for the youth who tried to tell the story from their own memory in Option A of "Telling the Story" to discover how we tend to combine both stories into one picture. After each group has had a chance to look at the differences between the two stories, gather the group back together and talk about the differences and similarities.

OPTION B

If you chose Option B under "Connecting to the Story" above, you may want to choose the following exercise for this segment.
Needed: "www.birthofchrist.com" handouts, Bible study materials
Provide the youth with biblical commentaries, maps, and other Bible study materials. Ask them to develop one of the areas of their website with further information from these resources. Suggest that they examine the political issues surrounding the birth of Jesus, talk more about what it was like to be a shepherd at the time of Jesus' birth, or include a picture suggesting what a stable would have been like in those times. After each person has had some time to look up further information on the topic that interests him or her most, have all the participants share at least one fact that they learned that was new to them. Go around the group until everyone has had a chance to share some of their new knowledge.

Living the Story
(5–10 minutes)

OPTION A
Needed: art supplies such as construction paper, markers, scissors, glitter, glue
Invite the youth to make paper angels. These may be as simple or as elaborate as time allows. About five minutes before your session is scheduled to end, ask the youth to finish their angels. Then ask them to think about a place where the news of the birth of Jesus needs to be proclaimed or about a person they know who needs to hear this

good news. Ask the youth to write the name of the place on the angel or, if they are thinking of a specific person, to write "a friend" rather than a specific name. Gather in a circle. Ask the participants who are willing to do so to share what they have written. Close with a time of prayer, praying especially that the good news of the birth of Jesus be proclaimed wherever people need to hear it.

OPTION B

Needed: small notebooks for the youth to use as journals
As you close this session, ask the youth to talk about what they learned about the birth of Jesus. Ask them to think about this question: "Are you ready to celebrate the birth of Jesus?" Remind the youth that this is different from being ready for Christmas and that it is a question that can be asked at any time of the year. Ask them to choose a number from one to ten that represents how prepared they feel right now for the celebration of Jesus' birth. Allow youth who are willing to share the number they chose.

Remind the youth that one way to get ready for the birth of Jesus is to spend more time in prayer and reflection. Distribute notebooks to the youth and ask them to use them as journals in the coming week. Encourage them to write a brief prayer each day. Ask them also to record any dreams they have and to take note of decisions they make during the week and what motivates them to make those decisions. Suggest that they write these three words in the front of their journals as reminders of what to write: prayer, dreams, decisions.

Close the session by singing a favorite Christmas carol that announces the birth of Jesus to all the world.

Things to Ponder

Talking about Christmas traditions may be uncomfortable for youth who are facing difficult family circumstances such as divorce, recent loss of a loved one, or financial strain. If you know the youth well, you may be aware of some of these situations and may be able to predict their comfort level with the discussion. Adjust your conversation as necessary. If someone does not want to talk about Christmas, do not force him or her to do so. Also, be aware that a diverse group will bring diverse customs and preferences with them. Foster an environment in which different traditions are respected.

Looking Ahead

If you choose "Living the Story," Option B from this session, you will give each youth a small notepad or journal. In the next session, the youth will have an opportunity to discuss the influences that motivate them to make certain decisions or do certain things. You might want to phone or e-mail youth during the week to remind them to keep their journals and to encourage them to bring them to the next session.

The Best Christmas Ever

You may not have a lot of say about Christmas traditions at your home right now. But someday, you'll be in charge. What will you do then? Tell us.

When should the Christmas tree go up?
  a. before Thanksgiving
  b. soon after Thanksgiving
  c. sometime between Thanksgiving and Christmas
  d. Christmas Eve
  e. whenever we get around to it

What kind of tree do you want?
  a. evergreen that we chop ourselves
  b. evergreen chopped by others and shipped on a truck
  c. artificial evergreen from a box
  d. potted tree that we can replant after Christmas
  e. other (white, pink, purple, fiber optic, and so on)

Who should put it up (or put it together)?
  a. adults only
  b. kids only
  c. everybody who is willing to help

Where do Christmas lights belong?
  a. only on the tree
  b. on the tree and in the windows
  c. on the tree, in the windows, and on a few outdoor plants
  d. everywhere!

What kind of Christmas lights do you prefer?
  a. multicolored
  b. clear
  c. candles
  d. icicles

What is your favorite kind of Christmas decorations?
  a. handmade: paper chains, popcorn strings, macaroni angels
  b. sentimental: family heirlooms, ornaments I made when I was a kid
  c. natural: pine cones, evergreen, holly
  d. stuff from a store

www.birthofchrist.com

16. We Have Seen His Star
Bible Story: Matthew 2:1–23

A Story behind the Story

The story of the magi and Herod in Matthew 2 has little in common with the birth story found in Luke's Gospel. Our Christmas customs have combined these two narratives to make one harmonious story, but that is not what the writers had in mind at all. Have you ever seen both shepherds and the magi in the nativity scene together? In Matthew's Gospel, the scene is filled with royalty, chief priests, and wealthy foreigners while the scene in Luke is a manger and simple shepherds. The images used in these stories reflect the authors' intended message of the story.

The magi play an important part in the first section of this session's Scripture (vv. 1–12). The word *magi* is translated from the Greek as "wise men" or "astrologers." They were most likely wealthy men from Persia or Babylon, not kings. Note also that there is no mention of the number of magi. Because they brought three gifts, many have assumed that there were three men, but the text is not clear. These men, who were Gentiles, were cast as the heroes of the story while Herod, a Jew, serves as the villain against the kingdom of God. The magi were obedient to the star and to the Scripture so that they might find the newborn king and worship him. Not only did the wise men listen to God but they also acted upon what God asked them to do. They provide the model for faithfulness and obedience.

The faithfulness of the magi is matched by the faithfulness of Joseph. In the first section (vv.1–12), the obedient magi encountered a rebellious Herod who wanted to kill the new king. They followed the star to Bethlehem and received a final warning against Herod in a dream. In verses 13–23, an obedient Joseph stands in stark contrast to the picture of an evil Herod. Joseph wanted to protect the child, while Herod would kill hundreds of children in his attempt to do away with the new king. Joseph followed the revelation of an angel and received his final warning about Herod in a dream.

Enter the Story

Before reading this story, sing or listen to a song about the magi, such as the carol "We Three Kings" or even James Taylor's song "Home by Another Way." After singing or listening to the song, offer a prayer asking God to guide you in this story just as God guided the magi to Jesus.

Read Matthew 2:1–23. Try to imagine the scenes presented in this story in rich detail. How are the magi dressed? How do they look and smell after their long journey? Imagine the conversations that must have taken place but are not presented here. How did Joseph explain to Mary that they were moving to Egypt? What did the soldiers say to the families as the children were killed?

This story is filled with joy, relief, sadness, and horror. Be aware of your own emotions as you work through it, and prepare yourself to discover similar reactions in the youth. Pray for God's guidance as you share this familiar yet surprising story.

Setting the Stage (10–15 minutes)

Check in with the group as they come into your meeting space by asking, "How is school? How was your week?" Check up on any prayer requests from last week. Then have the group answer a question such as, "What was the best Christmas present you ever received? How old were you? Why was it the very best?"

OPTION A

Needed: materials for making magi costumes and gifts—cloth for headbands, towels and robes to simulate the dress of the magi—old boxes, bottles, fabric, jewelry, and other craft materials for gifts

Invite the youth to dress like one of the magi. Have prepared for them strips of cloth for headbands, fabric to simulate robes, jewels, and so on. Direct the youth to a table containing old boxes, bottles, fabric, jewelry, and other craft materials. Ask each youth to create a gift for the Christ child. They can decide what the gift might contain and in what form they would choose to present it to Jesus. After the group has had a few minutes to make the gifts, gather the group in a circle and have each person present his or her gift. As the youth present their gifts, ask them to share what they are and how they made their decisions about what to bring.

OPTION B

Needed: portable stereo and tapes or CDs of Christmas music, a small gift that is wrapped many times with lots of tape

Play a game called "Musical Gift Unwrap." Before the session begins, take a small toy or prize and wrap it up with lots of paper, ribbon, and tape. Make it difficult to get into and hard to unwrap. Have the group sit in a circle. Give the gift to someone in the circle and explain to the youth that as the music plays, they should hand the gift around the circle from person to person until the music stops. Whoever has the gift when the music stops should try to unwrap it as fast as possible, until the music starts again, and then the gift must continue on around the circle. Each time the music stops, someone gets to try to unwrap it, so that the gift is being unwrapped a little at a time. Play the music, stopping it at short intervals. Make the time each person is unwrapping the gift short so that only a little progress is made every turn. When someone succeeds in totally unwrapping the gift, award the gift to that person as a prize.

Telling the Story (10–15 minutes)

OPTION A

Needed: twelve stars, flashlights, Bibles

Before the session begins, prepare twelve stars. If possible, use glow-in-the-dark plastic stars or cut simple ones from bright construction paper. Number the stars from one to twelve. Write the following Scripture references on the stars:

POSSIBLE YOUTH CONTACT POINTS
- Why do bad things happen?
- Where is God leading me?
- What gifts do I have to bring?
- Am I looking for Jesus?
- What signs do I see along the way?

YOU MAY NEED
- cloth for headbands, towels and robes to simulate the dress of the magi
- old boxes, bottles, fabric, jewelry, and other craft materials for gifts
- small gift wrapped many times with lots of tape
- portable stereo and tapes or CDs of Christmas music
- twelve glow-in-the-dark plastic stars or paper stars, plus one more for each youth
- flashlights
- Bibles
- large sheets of paper cut in the shape of stars with questions written on them
- markers
- "Bible Christmas Quiz" handouts
- pencils
- small notebooks for journals
- Bible study materials such as commentaries, dictionary, concordance
- "Three Gifts" handouts
- magazines, catalogs, scissors, envelopes
- permanent markers

- Star 1: Matthew 2:1–2
- Star 2: Matthew 2:3–4
- Star 3: Matthew 2:5–6
- Star 4: Matthew 2:7–8
- Star 5: Matthew 2:9–10
- Star 6: Matthew 2:11–12
- Star 7: Matthew 2:13
- Star 8: Matthew 2:14–15
- Star 9: Matthew 2:16–18
- Star 10: Matthew 2:19–20
- Star 11: Matthew 2:21–22
- Star 12: Matthew 2:23

Prior to the session, hang the stars randomly around the room. If possible, use a hallway or other rooms that might be available.

Form small groups and give each group a flashlight. Darken the room and tell the groups that they are to search for stars hidden in the room. When they find a star, they should take it and keep looking until all twelve stars are found. When all of the stars have been discovered, turn on the lights and give a Bible to each group. Ask the group that found Star 1 to read the verses printed on it, and then have the groups keep reading aloud in order until the entire story has been read.

OPTION B
Needed: Bibles
Form two groups, one to read or act out the story found in Matthew 2:1–23, and the other to provide sound effects. Allow the youth to choose which group they want to join. Give the groups about five minutes to prepare their presentations. Instruct the reading/acting group to assign parts and to use the words that are printed in the text. Ask the sound effects group to decide which sounds to make

during different parts of the story. Tell them they may consider using sounds like background music and melodramatic effects such as booing when bad things happen in the story, cheering when good things happen, making special noises such as a trumpet flourish when God speaks, and so on.

When the groups are ready, ask them to present the Scripture story. Encourage the youth to laugh and have fun with this activity.

Reacting to the Story (5–10 minutes)
OPTION A
Needed: large sheets of construction paper or newsprint cut in the shape of stars with questions written on them, markers
Prior to the session, write questions about the story on the stars. After reading or telling the story, hang these around the room. Place markers near the stars. Invite youth to choose two or three questions to answer. Allow about five minutes for youth to go to the stars and write their answers on them. You may use the following questions, along with others of your own. The purpose of these questions is to invite the youth to think about what happened in the story.

- Had you heard this story before?
- What surprised you this time?
- Why did the magi want to find Jesus?
- Why did Herod want to kill Jesus?
- How did God communicate with people in this story?
- Who was the bravest person in this story?

OPTION B

Needed: "Bible Christmas Quiz" handouts, pencils, Bibles

Invite youth to take the Bible Christmas Quiz. Distribute the handouts and pencils. Tell the youth they may work in pairs or by themselves to answer the questions, but they may not use their Bibles. Ask them to answer the questions in the quiz on the basis of what they remember hearing in the story. After everyone has had a chance to answer all the questions, gather the group back together. Beginning with Question 1, ask the youth how they responded to each question. After all youth have responded, reveal the correct answers and invite youth to find Scripture verses that clarify them. The answers are as follows: 1. d [the Bible does not call them kings], 2. a [they came to Jesus' house and not to the manger], 3. b, 4. a, 5. c, 6. b, 7. b, 8. d, 9. b, 10. c. Spend a few minutes discussing each of the questions. If youth have other questions about the story encourage them to talk about these now.

Connecting to the Story (10 to 15 minutes)

OPTION A

Needed: large sheets of paper cut in the shape of stars, markers

This activity is similar to Option A in "Reacting to the Story," but here the youth will answer questions about how they relate to this story. Prior to the session, prepare several large stars and write a different question on each sheet. To begin the activity, post the stars around the room and place markers near the stars. Ask the youth to find a star that has a question on it that they would like to answer. When they finish, invite them to answer additional questions. Allow about five minutes. Bring the youth back together and discuss their responses. Use the following questions, or pose some of your own:

■ Why do you think the magi followed the star?

■ What are some signs that you have followed that have shown you the way to Jesus?

■ In your journey toward God, how have you been like the magi? Unlike them?

■ Have you been frightened on your journey? When and why?

■ What gifts are you bringing to Jesus?

■ How does God speak to you?

OPTION B

Needed: small notebooks to use as journals, pencils

"Living the Story," Option B, from the previous session suggested giving journals to the youth and asking them to record influences that motivated them to make certain decisions. If the youth kept journals during the past week, refer to them now. Try to have a few extra journals on hand for those who were not there the week before or for those who forgot their journals. If the youth have not had a chance to work on the assignment, allow a few minutes for writing. Ask them to think about events from the previous week and write about the decisions they made and about what influenced them to make those decisions. Invite them to include any dreams that they remember from the past week. When you are ready for discussion, invite the youth to talk about the things they identified that motivate them. Help them discover what sorts of core values motivate their decisions. This is a good opportunity for you to share with the youth what your core values are and how you make decisions. You might also share about a time when you made a poor decision. Let the youth ask you some questions. Encourage them to continue their journals in the coming weeks.

Exploring the Story (10–15 minutes)

OPTION A

Needed: Bible study materials such as Bible commentaries or Bible dictionaries, paper, pencils
Invite the youth to learn more about some of the principal characters in this story, Herod and the magi. Form two groups by allowing the youth to select which character(s) they would like to study in greater detail. Give each group access to Bible study materials, paper, and pencils. Allow five to ten minutes for the groups to learn what they can about these characters. If they have trouble finding information, suggest that they look up key words in a Bible dictionary or read a commentary on this session's Scripture passage. After the groups have found their information, ask them to share what they have learned. As each group shares, ask the other group to respond. Ask questions such as:
- Are you surprised by this information?

- Does this information seem consistent with what we learned about these characters in the story?

OPTION B

Needed: "Three Gifts" handouts, pencils, Bible concordance, Bible dictionary, Bible commentaries
Distribute "Three Gifts" handouts, pencils, and the Bible study materials. Ask the youth to discover more information about the gifts the magi brought to Jesus. If you need to save time, form three groups and ask each group to focus on one gift. There are several ways to find this information. Encourage the youth to read about this passage in a Bible commentary; most will have some information about the magi's gifts. Tell the participants they may look up the words or parts of these words in a concordance and learn how these objects are used in other parts of Scripture. They may need to look up "incense" rather than "frankincense" and "ointment" rather than "myrrh." They may also look up these words in a Bible dictionary. Ask them to answer all the questions on the handout. When groups have finished, talk together about what they learned. Ask, "What do these gifts tell us about how the magi understood Jesus?"

If time permits, encourage the youth to turn to the back of the handout and write a thank-you note from Mary and Joseph to the magi. Help them get started by asking questions such as:
- What would they say?
- How might they thank the magi for these gifts?

**Living the Story
(5–10 minutes)**

OPTION A

Needed: a glow-in-the-dark or brightly colored star for each youth, permanent markers

Give the youth each a glow-in-the-dark star. Ask them to write their names on the stars with a permanent marker. Ask them also to write one area in their lives in which they need to receive guidance from God. When they are finished writing, put the stars into a basket and invite each person to draw one star out. Make sure that no one gets his or her own star. After all the stars have been drawn, have the youth pair up with the person who has drawn their star and then pair up with the person whose star they drew. Have each pair talk in more detail about the situations for which they seek God's guidance. After the pairs have had a chance to share with each other, invite each youth to take the star home and put it in a place where they will see it each day, like the bathroom mirror. Ask them to begin praying for their star prayer partners. Close in prayer, seeking God's guidance in life.

OPTION B

Needed: magazines, catalogs, scissors, envelopes

Invite the youth to participate in a gift exchange for the Christ Child. Give newspaper ads and catalogs to the youth and ask them to cut out pictures of items that could be given to Jesus. Remind them that one way to give to Jesus is to give to others who are in need. Invite each youth to choose a gift from the catalogs or magazines, cut it out, and place it in an envelope. When all of the participants have done this, have them take turns opening the envelopes and explaining how their gifts could be used. For example, someone may cut out a picture of athletic shoes and tell about a child at school who needs some new shoes. After all the envelopes have been opened, go around the circle and ask each youth to name one gift that he or she can give Christ this week. This should not be an actual item but rather a gift of time or activity. For example, they might clean their rooms without being asked or maybe bake some cookies for a elderly neighbor. Close the time with prayer, thanking God for the gifts we are given and for the gift of the Christ Child.

Things to Ponder

Some difficult issues may surface during this session. Child abuse is a potential topic of discussion; be sensitive to those youth who have personally dealt with this issue. Another tough issue that many youth will struggle with is the question of why bad things happen to certain people and not to others. Be prepared to help youth deal with the struggle of being faithful in spite of difficult situations. Some youth may have a hard time dealing with these issues and emotions may run high. Make this be a safe place where all can share.

Bible Christmas Quiz

1. Who saw the star in the east?
   a. shepherds
   b. three kings
   c. the king
   d. none of the above

2. How many wise men came to see Jesus in the manger?
   a. 0
   b. 1
   c. 2
   d. 3

3. What is frankincense?
   a. an oriental spice
   b. a precious perfume
   c. a precious fabric
   d. a precious metal

4. What is myrrh?
   a. a spice used in burials
   b. a soft metal
   c. a drink
   d. a rare medicine

5. What does "wise men" refer to?
   a. men of the educated class
   b. Eastern kings
   c. astrologers
   d. fortune tellers

6. The wise men stopped in Jerusalem
   a. to find out where Jesus was.
   b. to ask about the star they saw.
   c. to inform Herod about Jesus.
   d. to buy presents for Jesus.

7. Why did Joseph take Jesus to Egypt?
   a. to show him the pyramids
   b. because he dreamed about it
   c. he never took Jesus there
   d. to be taxed

8. How long did Joseph, Mary, and Jesus live in Egypt?
   a. until Jesus grew up
   b. for just a few months
   c. forever
   d. until King Herod died

9. Who did Herod order to be killed in Bethlehem?
   a. all the babies in the land
   b. all the children under two years old
   c. all the first-born males

10. When Joseph returned to Israel, where did he choose to live?
    a. Bethlehem
    b. Jerusalem
    c. Nazareth
    d. Dan

Three Gifts

These were not your typical baby presents.

Gold

What is it?

What do you do with it?

Why would the magi give this to Jesus?

Frankincense

What is it?

What do you do with it?

Why would the magi give this to Jesus?

Myrrh

What is it?

What do you do with it?

Why would the magi give this to Jesus?